STAR WARS®

CLONE WARS

ADVENTURES

VOLUME 4

designer
Joshua Elliott

assistant editor
Dave Marshall

editor
Jeremy Barlow

publisher
Mike Richardson

special thanks to Sue Rostoni, Leland Chee, and Amy Gary at
Lucas Licensing

The events in this story take place
just before and during the events in
Star Wars: Episode III *Revenge of the Sith*

www.titanbooks.com
www.starwars.com

STAR WARS: CLONE WARS ADVENTURES Volume 4, October 2005. Published by Titan Books, a division of Titan Publishing Group Ltd., 144 Southwark Street, London SE1 0UP. Star Wars ©2005 Lucasfilm Ltd. & ™. All rights reserved. Used under authorization. Text and illustrations for Star Wars are © 2005 Lucasfilm Ltd. No portion of this publication may be reproduced or transmitted, in any form or by any means, without the express written permission of the copyright holder. Names, characters, places, and incidents featured in this publication either are the product of the author's imagination or are used fictitiously. Any resemblance to actual persons (living or dead), events, institutions, or locales, without satiric intent, is coincidental. PRINTED IN ITALY.

2 4 6 8 10 9 7 5 3

STAR WARS

CLONE WARS ADVENTURES

VOLUME 4

"ANOTHER FINE MESS"
script and art The Fillbach Brothers
colors Pamela Rambo

"THE BRINK"
script Justin Lambros
art Rick Lacy
colors Dan Jackson

"ORDERS"
script Ryan Kaufman
art The Fillbach Brothers
colors Ronda Pattison

"DESCENT"
script Haden Blackman
art The Fillbach Brothers
colors Dave Nestelle

lettering
Michael David Thomas

cover
The Fillbach Brothers and Dan Jackson

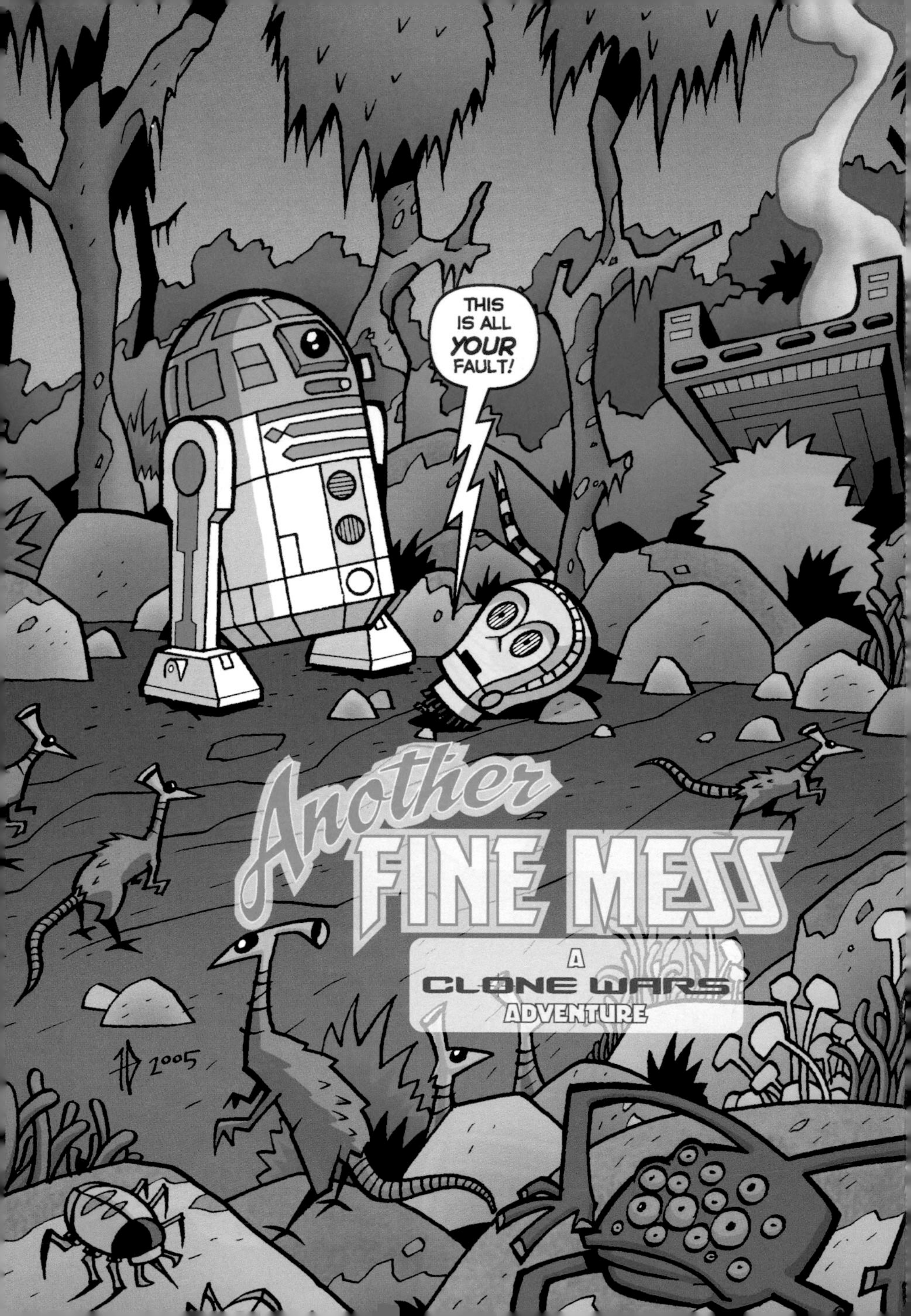
THIS IS ALL YOUR FAULT!
Another FINE MESS
A CLONE WARS ADVENTURE
2005

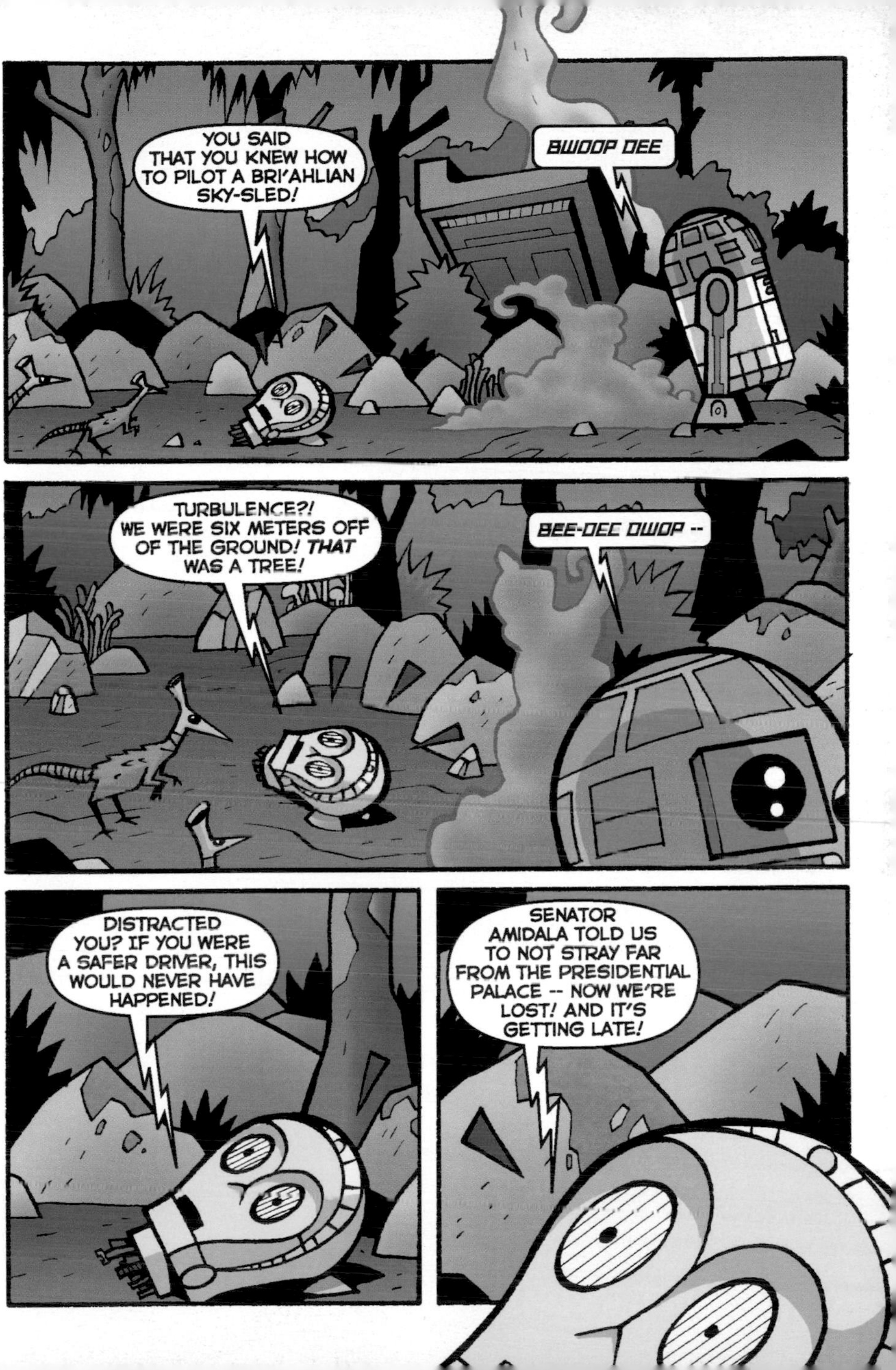
YOU SAID THAT YOU KNEW HOW TO PILOT A BRI'AHLIAN SKY-SLED!
BWOOP DEE
TURBULENCE?! WE WERE SIX METERS OFF OF THE GROUND! THAT WAS A TREE!
BEE-DEE DWOP --
DISTRACTED YOU? IF YOU WERE A SAFER DRIVER, THIS WOULD NEVER HAVE HAPPENED!
SENATOR AMIDALA TOLD US TO NOT STRAY FAR FROM THE PRESIDENTIAL PALACE -- NOW WE'RE LOST! AND IT'S GETTING LATE!

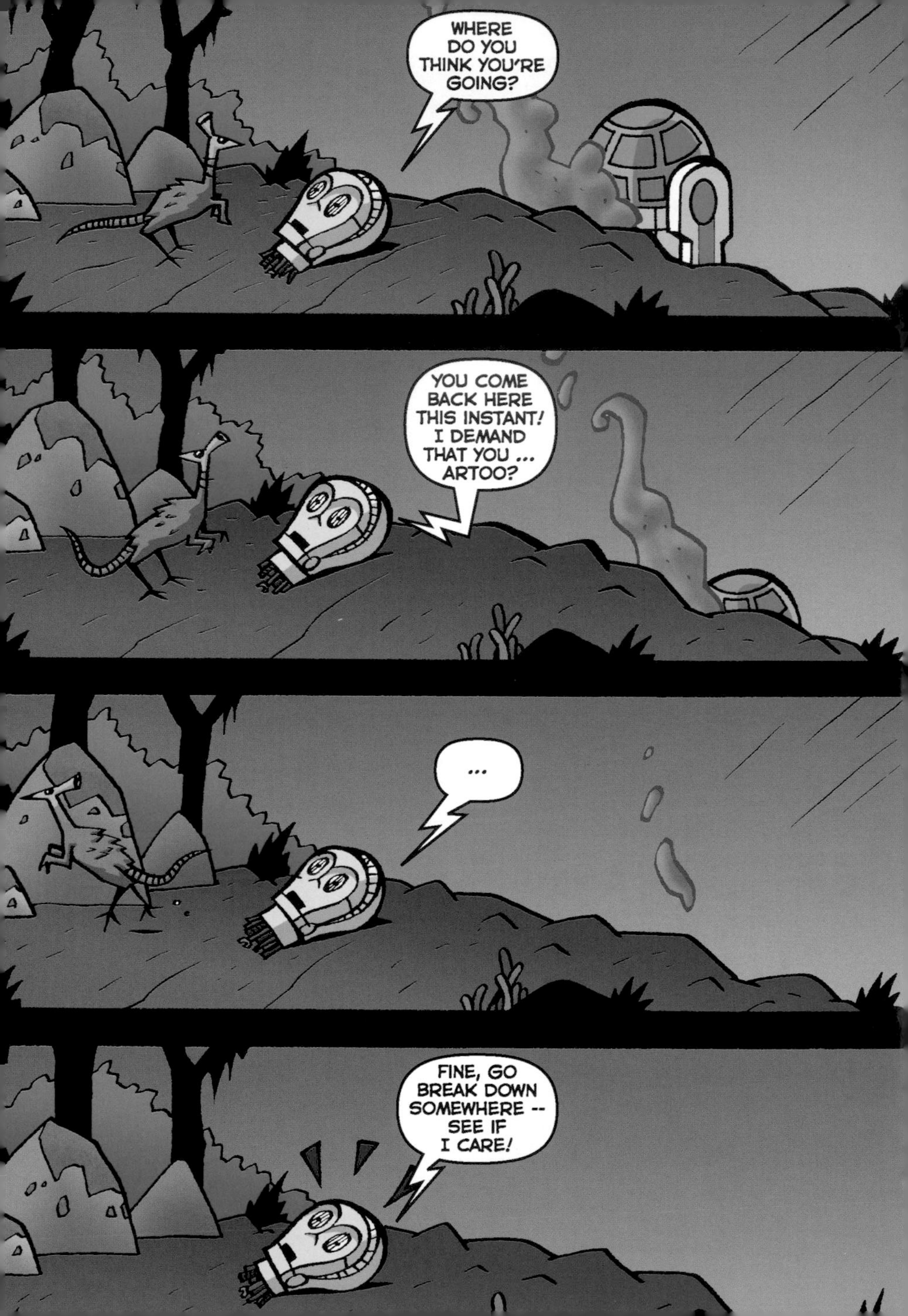
WHERE DO YOU THINK YOU'RE GOING?
YOU COME BACK HERE THIS INSTANT! I DEMAND THAT YOU ... ARTOO?
...
FINE, GO BREAK DOWN SOMEWHERE -- SEE IF I CARE!

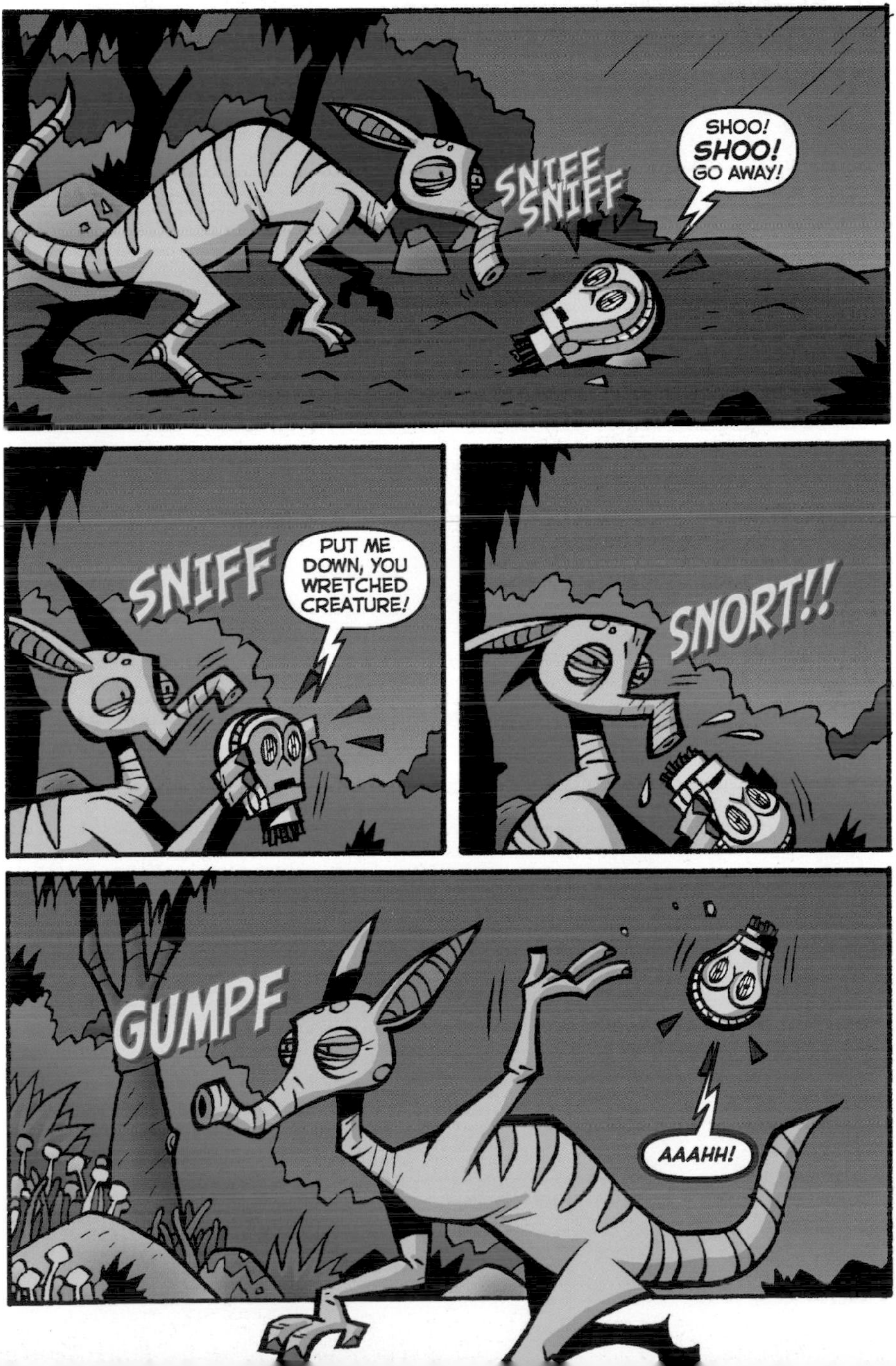
SNIFF SNIFF
SHOO! SHOO! GO AWAY!
SNIFF
PUT ME DOWN, YOU WRETCHED CREATURE!
SNORT!!
GUMPF
AAAHH!

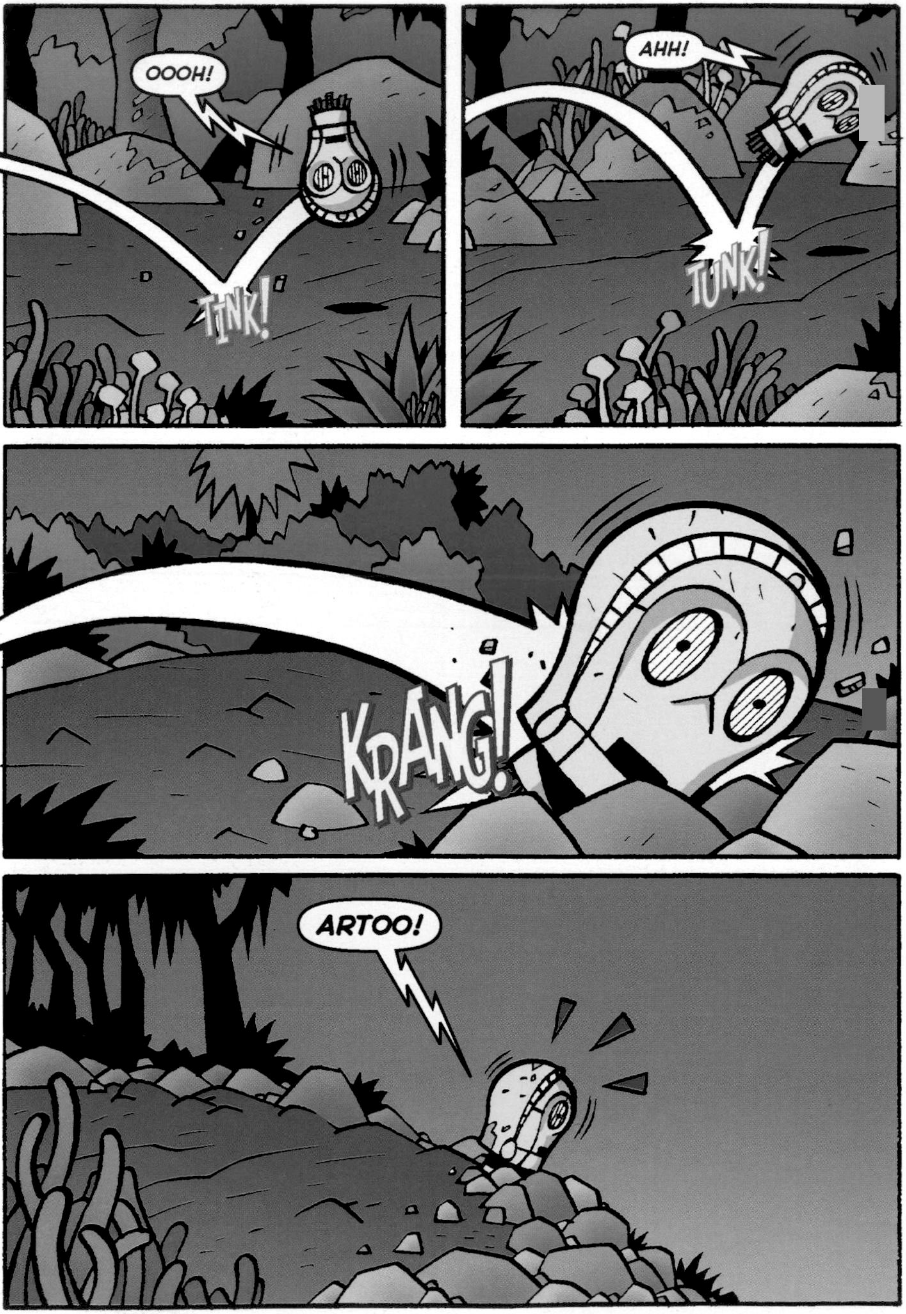
OOOH!
TINK!
AHH!
TUNK!
KRANG!
ARTOO!

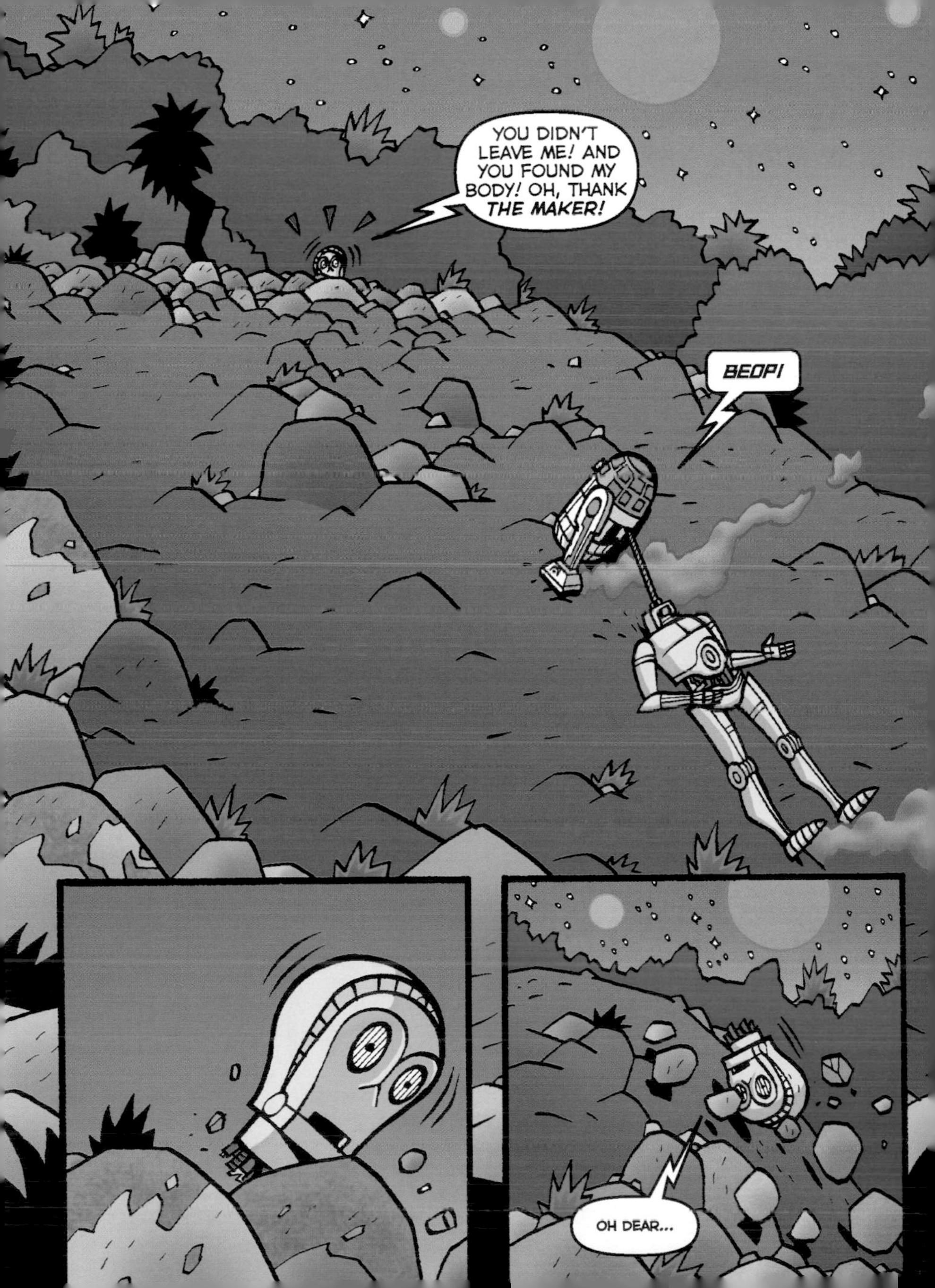
YOU DIDN'T LEAVE ME! AND YOU FOUND MY BODY! OH, THANK *THE MAKER!*
BEEP!
OH DEAR...

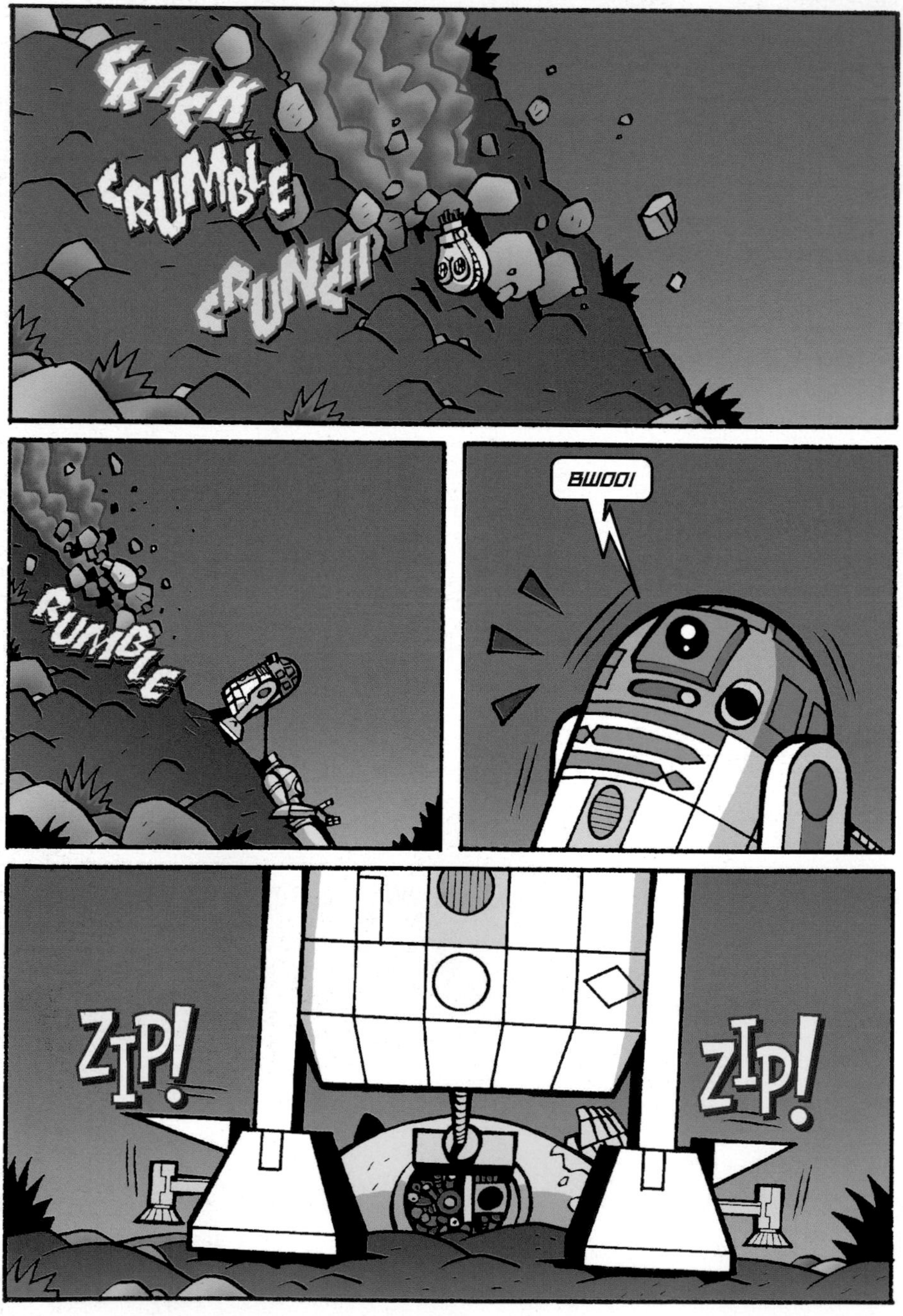
CRACK
CRUMBLE
CRUNCH
RUMBLE
BWOO!
ZIP!
ZIP!

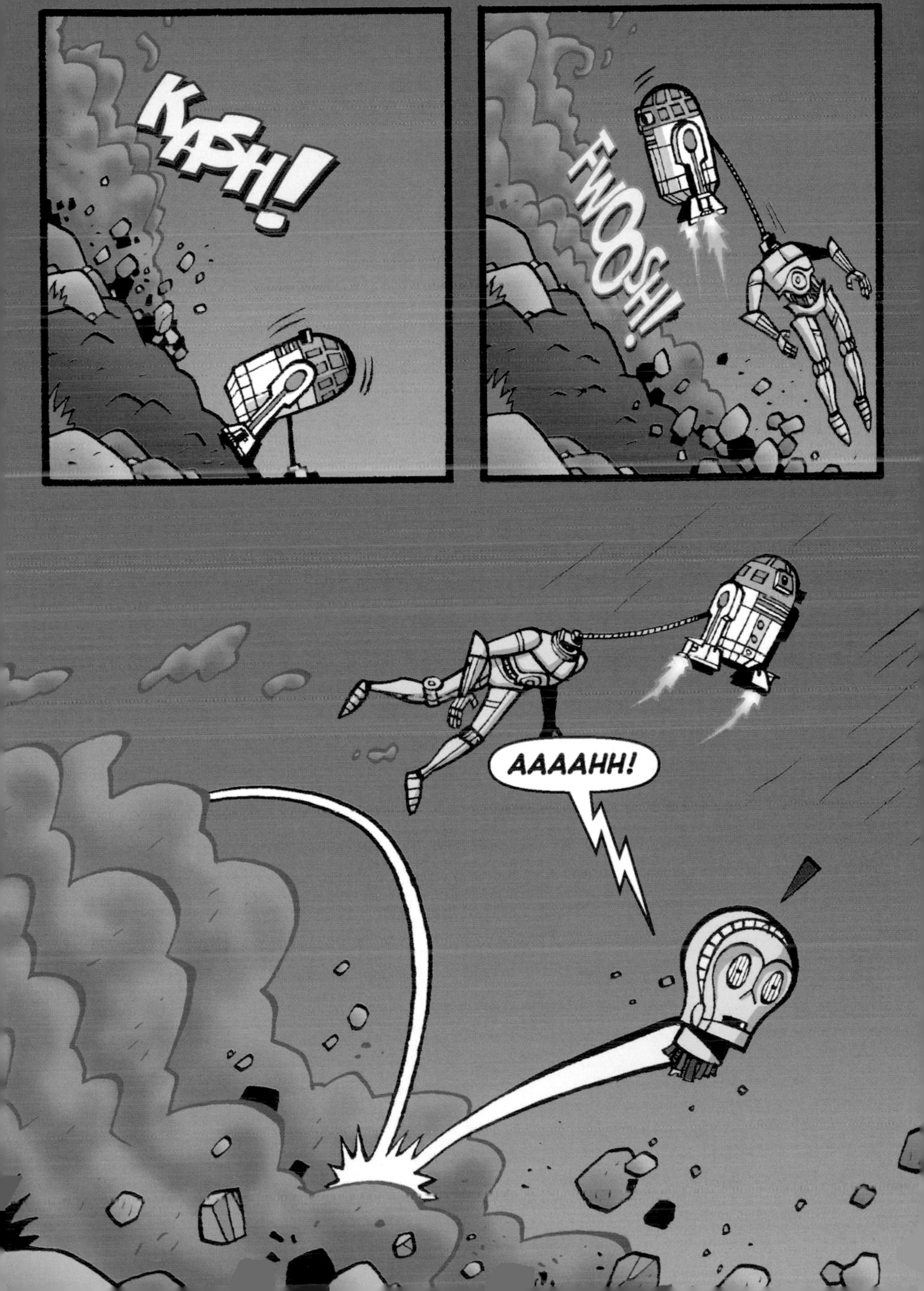

KASH!
FWOOSH!!
AAAAHH!

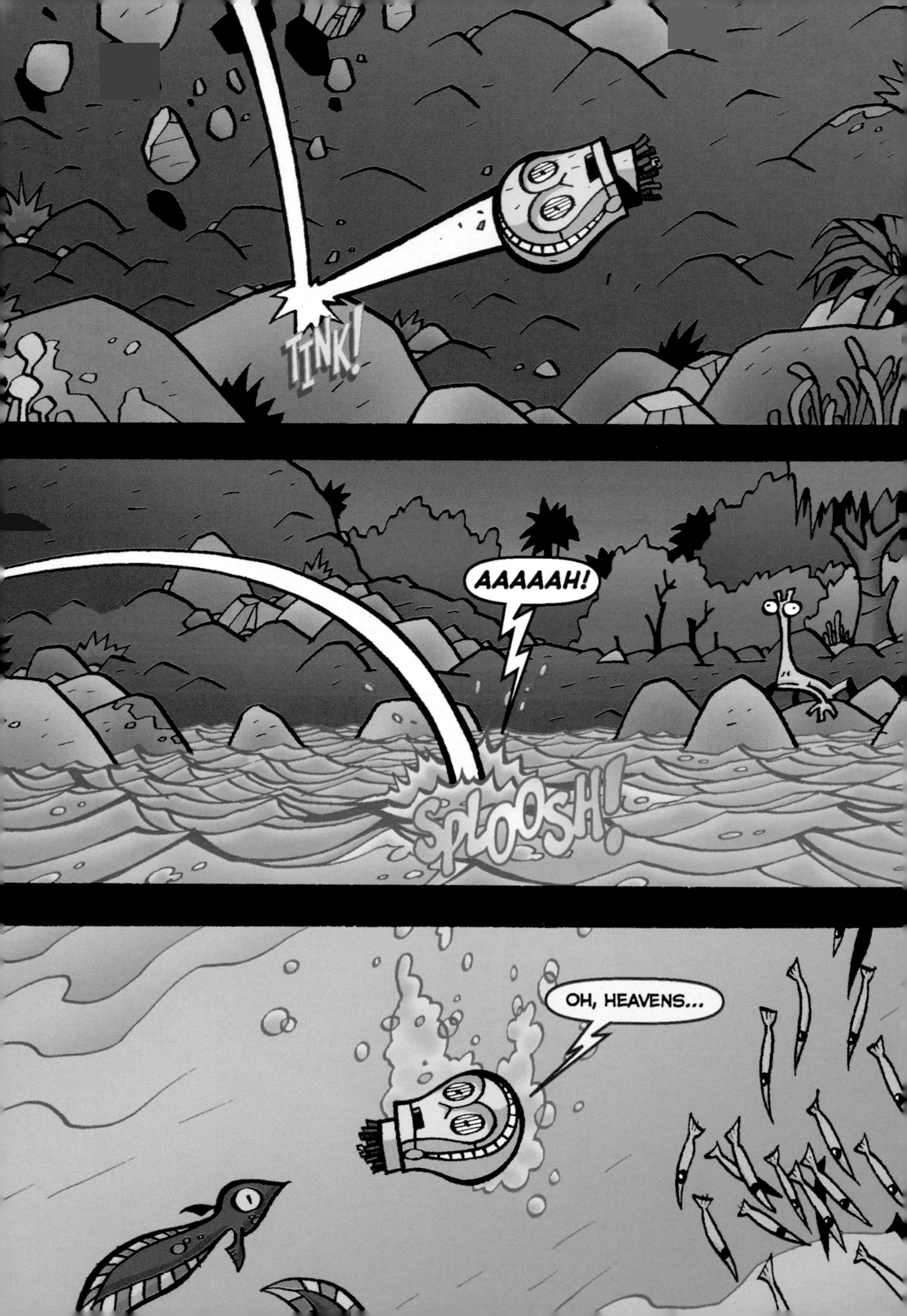
TINK!
AAAAAH!
SPLOOSH!
OH, HEAVENS...

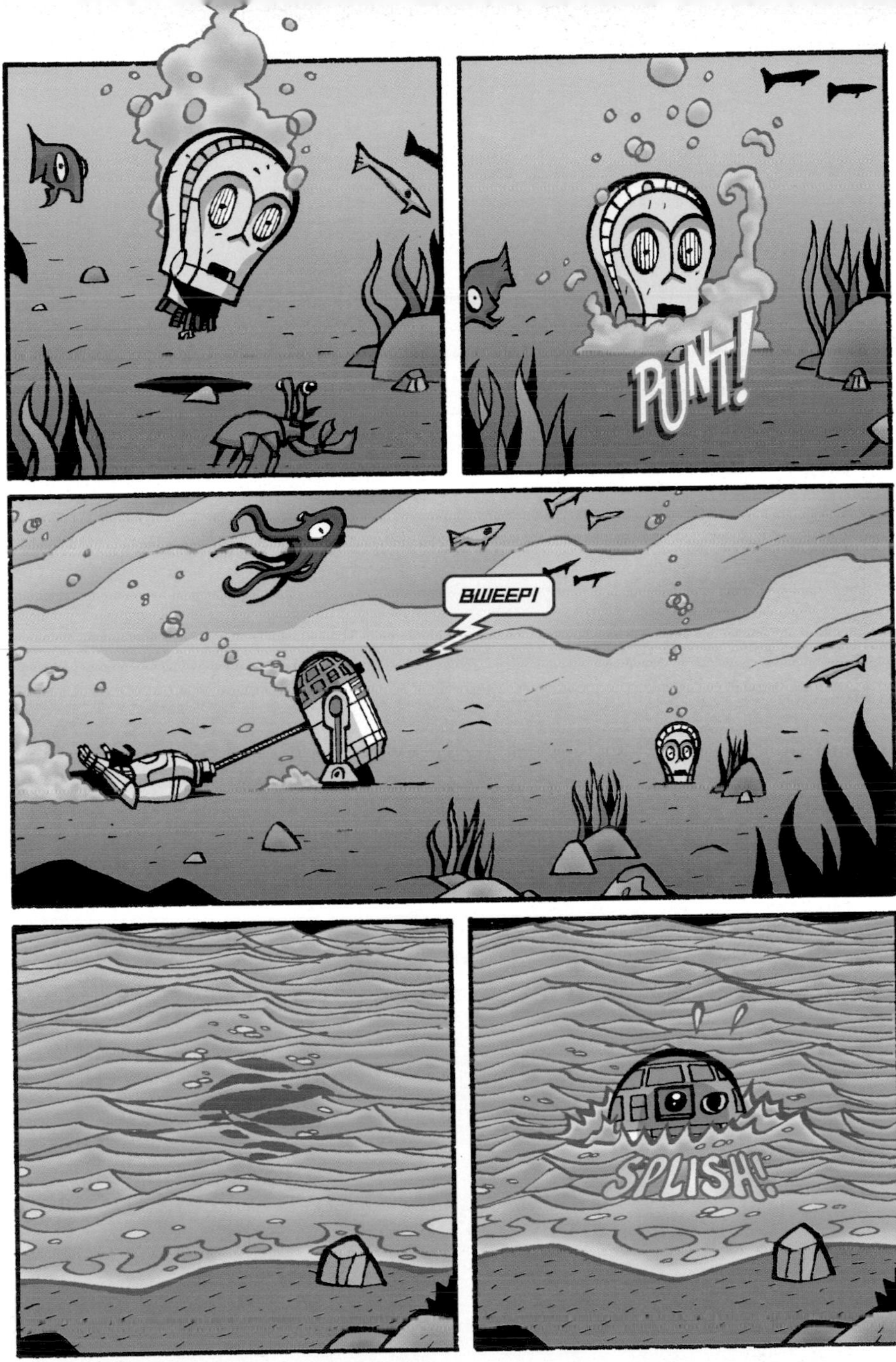
PUNT!
BWEEP!
SPLISH!

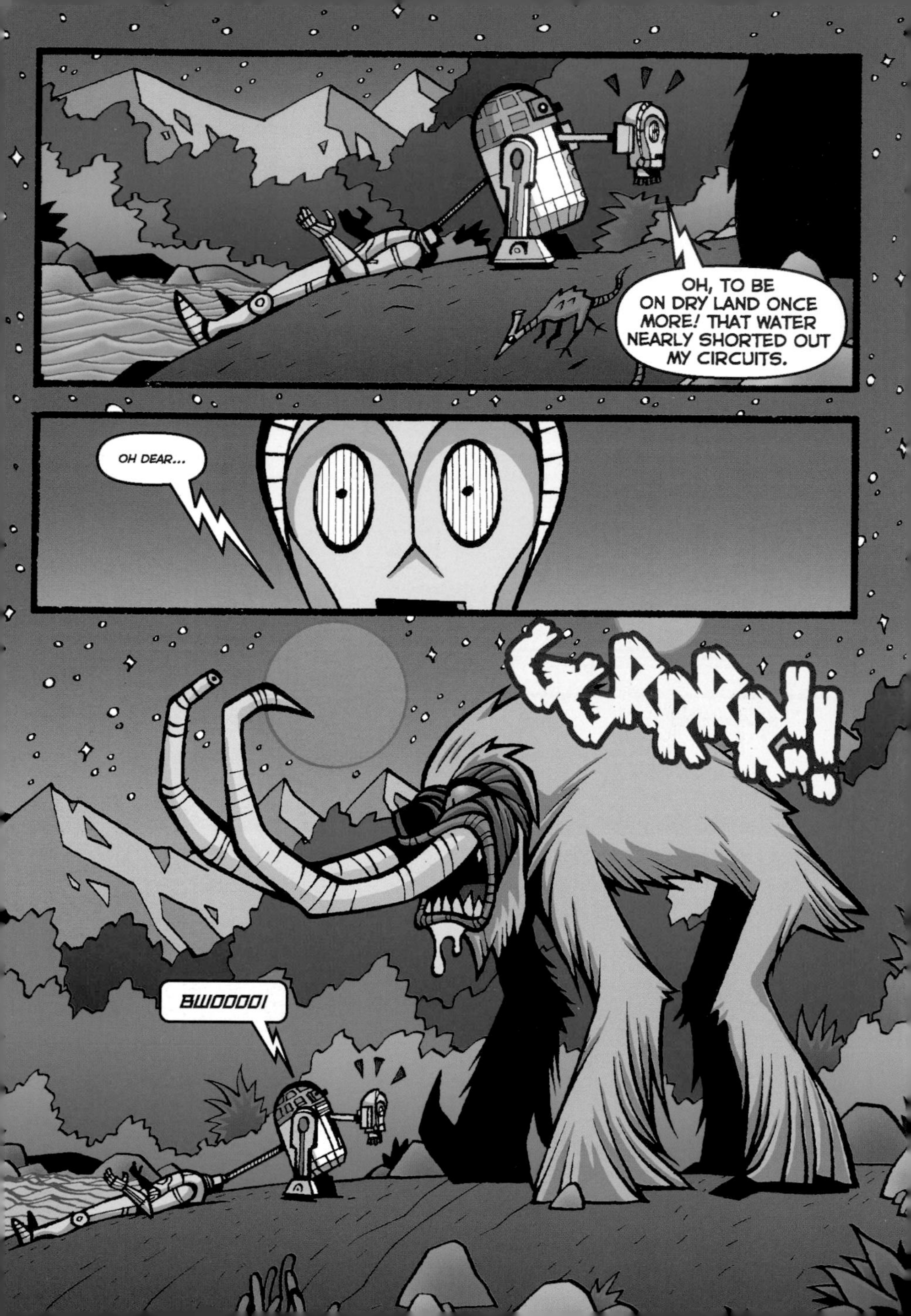
OH, TO BE ON DRY LAND ONCE MORE! THAT WATER NEARLY SHORTED OUT MY CIRCUITS.
OH DEAR...
GRRRR!!
BWOOOO!

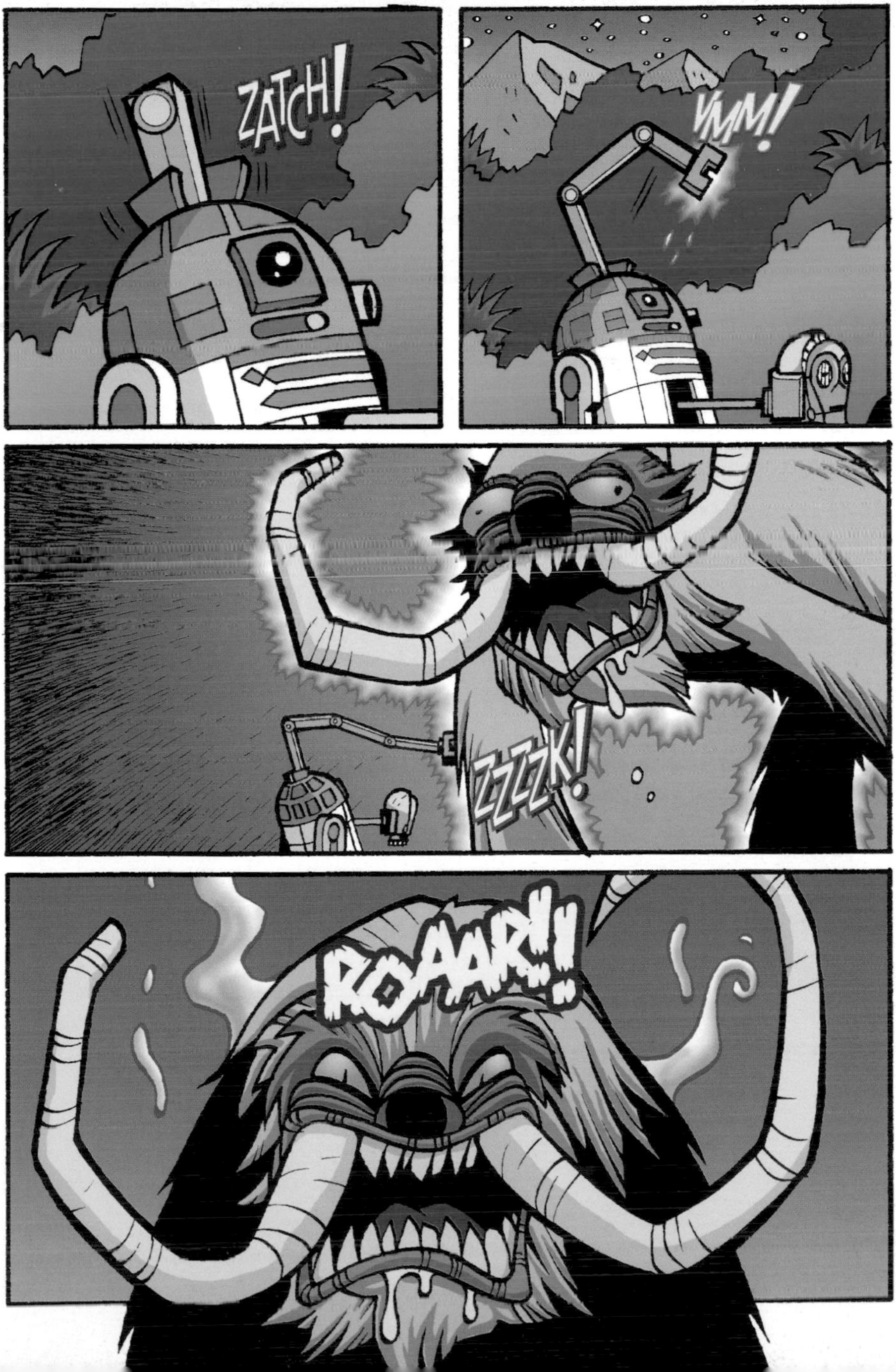
ZATCH!
VMM!
ZZZZK!
ROAAR!!

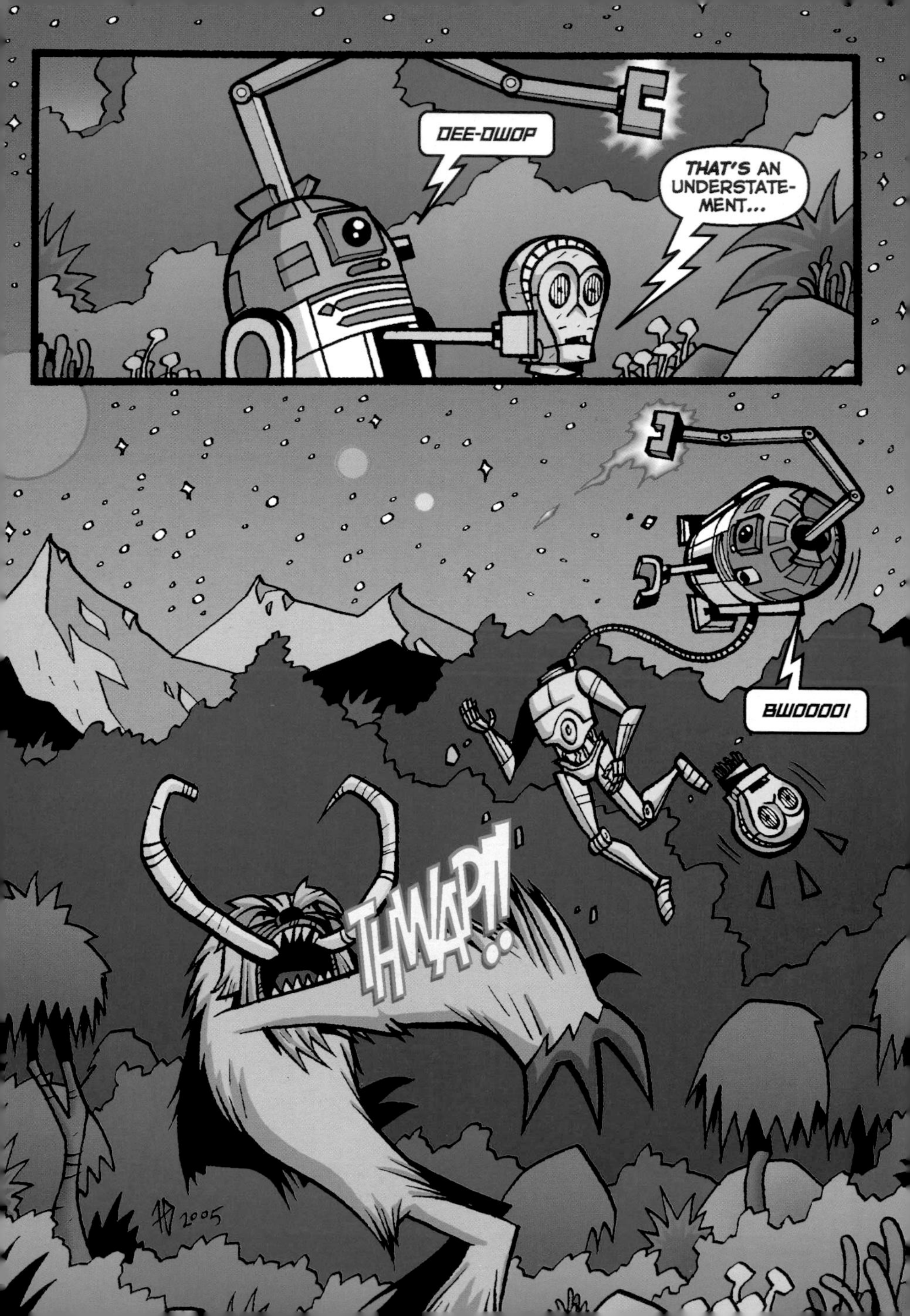
DEE-DWOP
THAT'S AN UNDERSTATE-MENT...
BWOOOOI
THWAP!!
2005

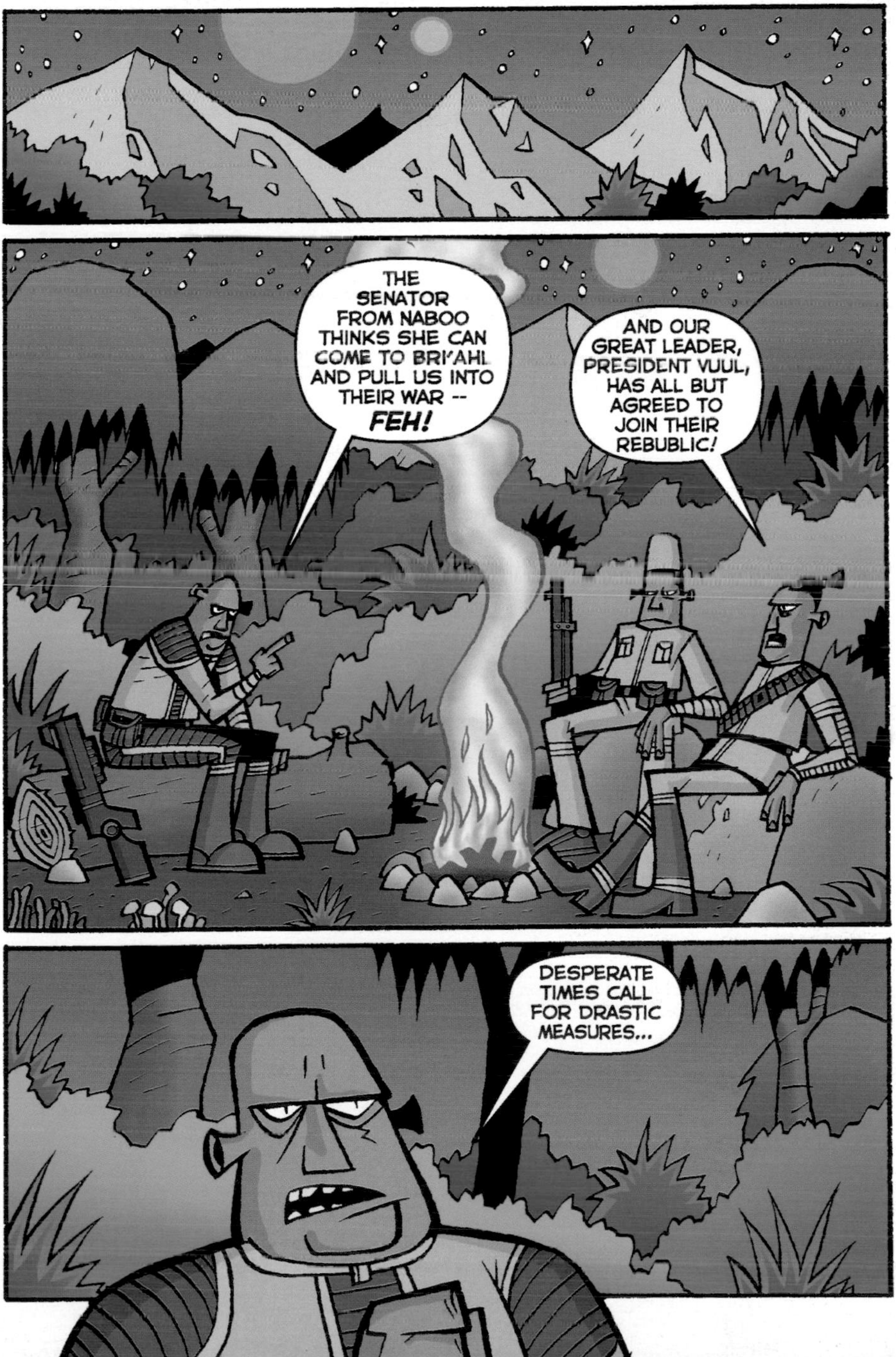
THE SENATOR FROM NABOO THINKS SHE CAN COME TO BRI'AHL AND PULL US INTO THEIR WAR -- FEH!
AND OUR GREAT LEADER, PRESIDENT VUUL, HAS ALL BUT AGREED TO JOIN THEIR REBUBLIC!
DESPERATE TIMES CALL FOR DRASTIC MEASURES...

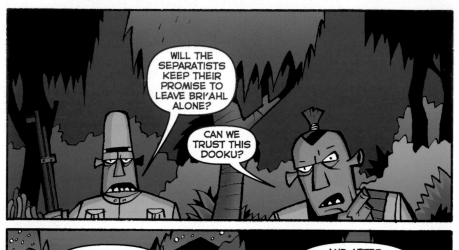

WILL THE SEPARATISTS KEEP THEIR PROMISE TO LEAVE BRI'AHL ALONE?

CAN WE TRUST THIS DOOKU?

COUNT DOOKU HAS EQUIPPED OUR MEN WITH THE CLONE TROOPER ARMOR AND WEAPONRY -- I HAVE NO REASON TO DOUBT HIS SINCERITY.

AND AFTER OUR MEN INFILTRATE THE PRESIDENTIAL PALACE AND ASSASSINATE BOTH THE NABOO SENATOR AND PRESIDENT VUUL, ALL OF BRI'AHL WILL *SEE* THAT THE REPUBLIC CANNOT BE TRUSTED.

IT'S TIME -- OUR MEN WILL BE WAITING IN THE FOREST ON THE EDGES OF THE PRESIDENTIAL PALACE GROUNDS. THE PALACE MONITORS ALL COMM TRANSMISSIONS, SO I'LL SIGNAL OUR MEN BY FLARE.

WE SHOULD BE ABLE TO HEAR THE THERMAL DETONATORS FROM HERE.

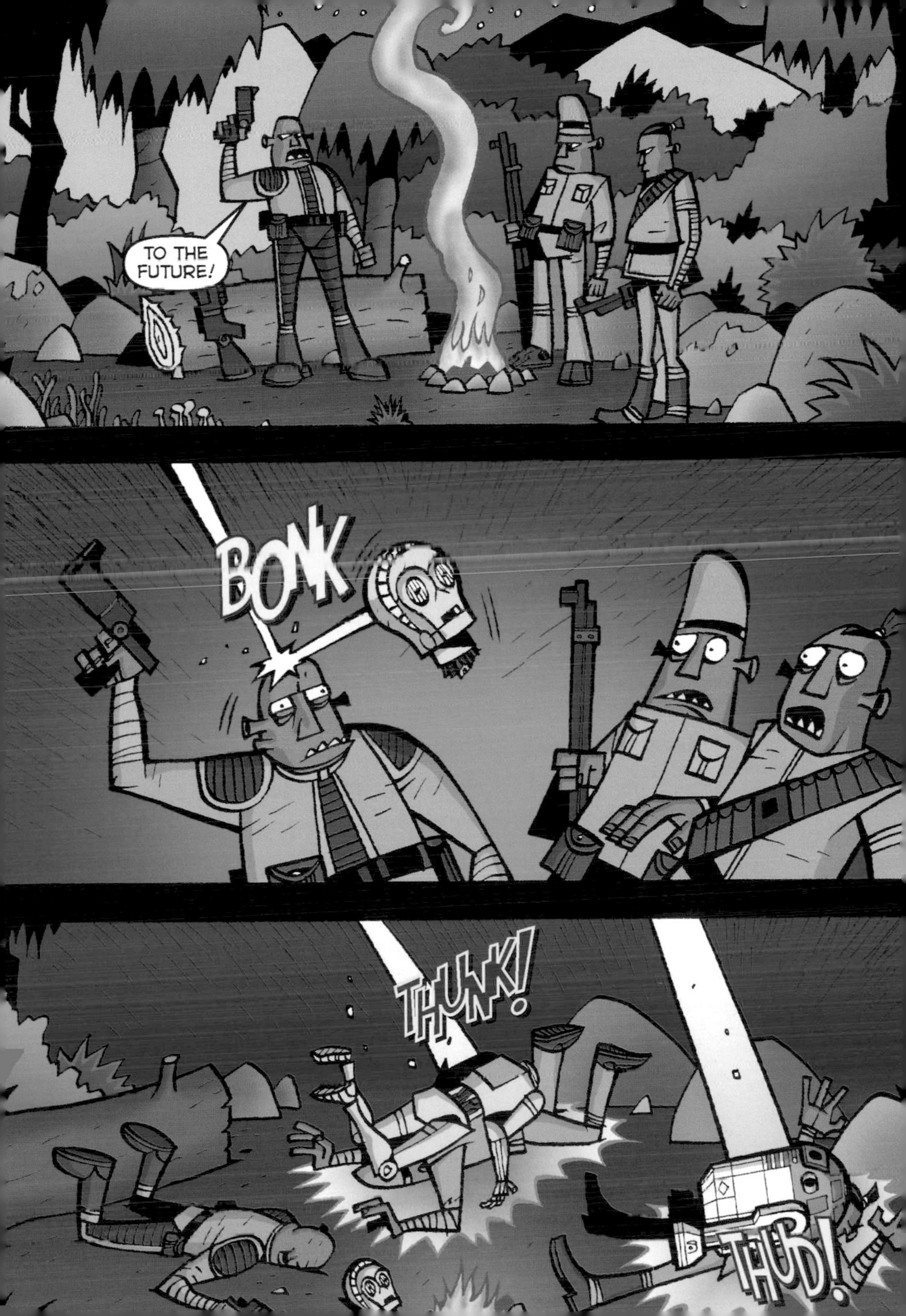
TO THE FUTURE!
BONK
THUNK!
THUD!

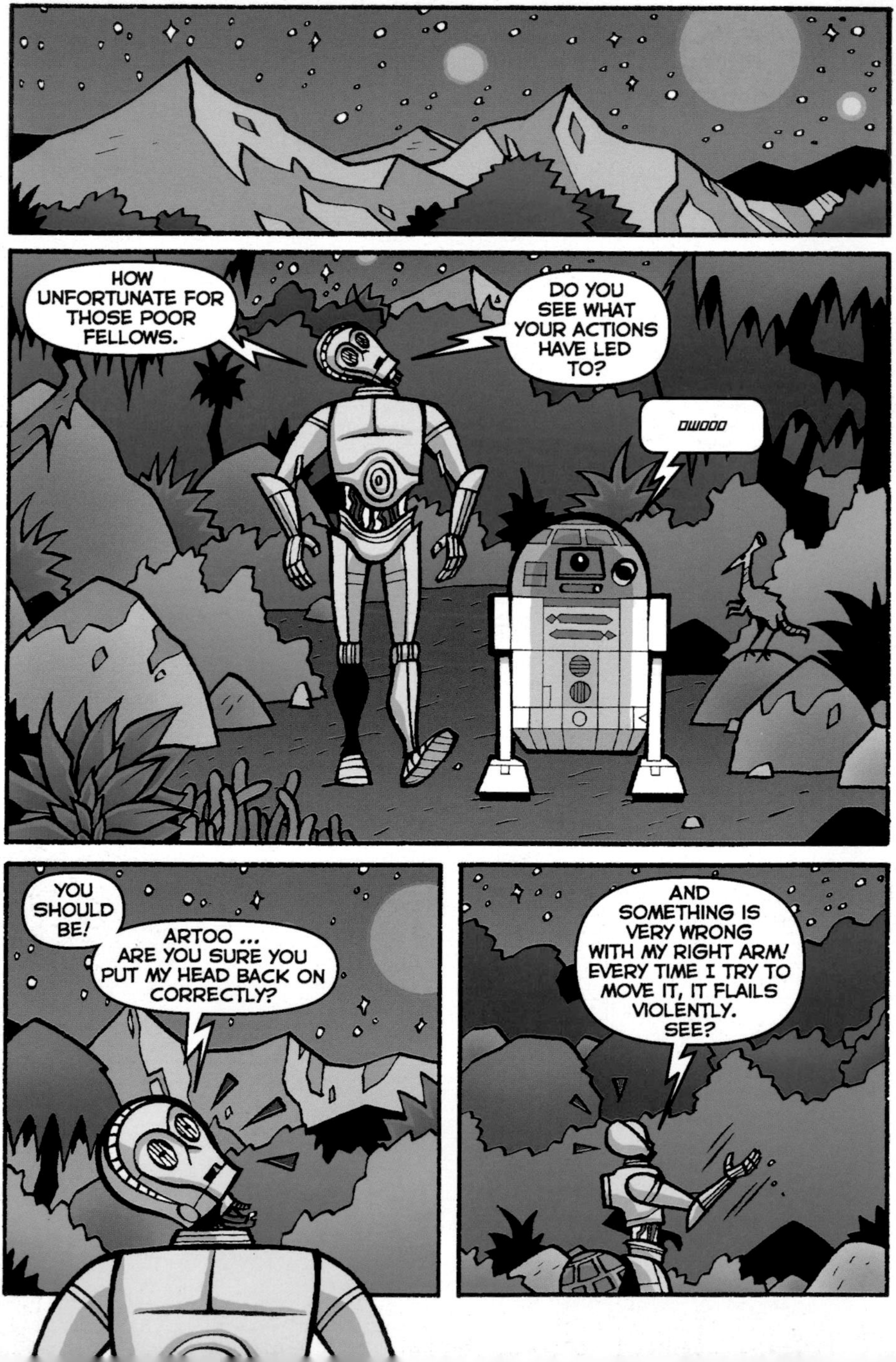
HOW UNFORTUNATE FOR THOSE POOR FELLOWS.
DO YOU SEE WHAT YOUR ACTIONS HAVE LED TO?
OWOOO
YOU SHOULD BE!
ARTOO ... ARE YOU SURE YOU PUT MY HEAD BACK ON CORRECTLY?
AND SOMETHING IS VERY WRONG WITH MY RIGHT ARM! EVERY TIME I TRY TO MOVE IT, IT FLAILS VIOLENTLY. SEE?

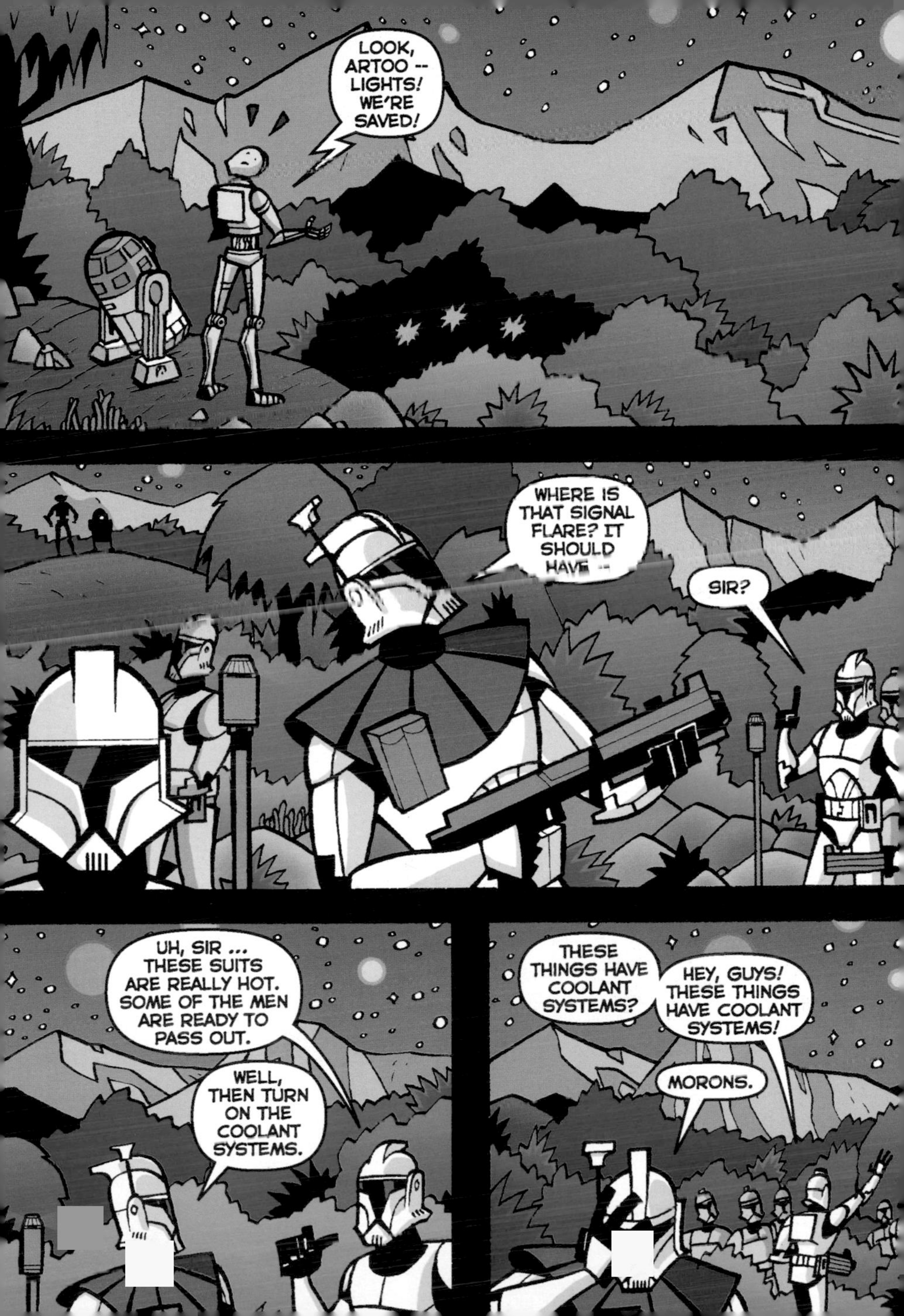
LOOK, ARTOO -- LIGHTS! WE'RE SAVED!
WHERE IS THAT SIGNAL FLARE? IT SHOULD HAVE --
SIR?
UH, SIR ... THESE SUITS ARE REALLY HOT. SOME OF THE MEN ARE READY TO PASS OUT.
WELL, THEN TURN ON THE COOLANT SYSTEMS.
THESE THINGS HAVE COOLANT SYSTEMS?
HEY, GUYS! THESE THINGS HAVE COOLANT SYSTEMS!
MORONS.

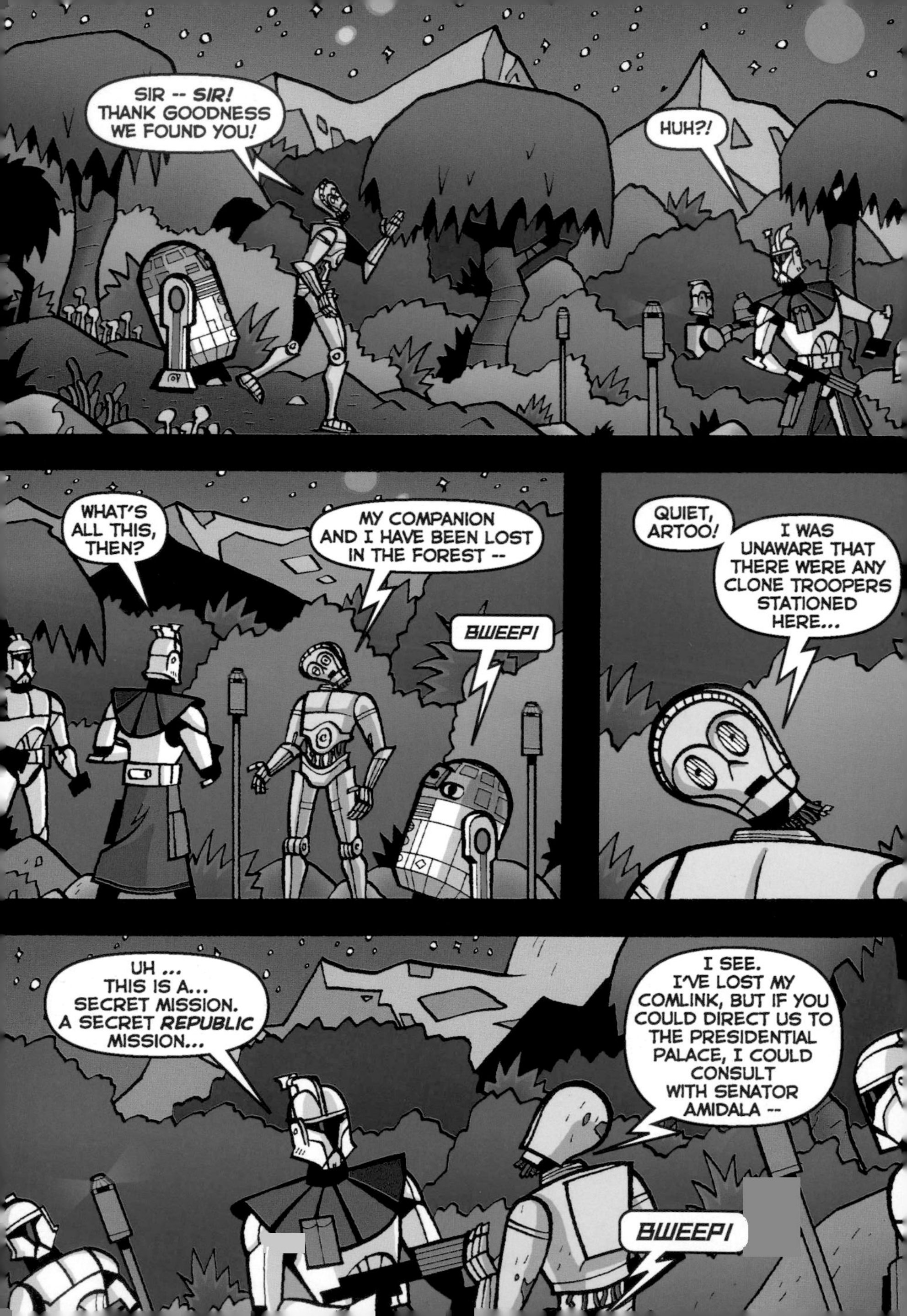
SIR -- *SIR!* THANK GOODNESS WE FOUND YOU!
HUH?!
WHAT'S ALL THIS, THEN?
MY COMPANION AND I HAVE BEEN LOST IN THE FOREST --
BWEEP!
QUIET, ARTOO!
I WAS UNAWARE THAT THERE WERE ANY CLONE TROOPERS STATIONED HERE...
UH ... THIS IS A... SECRET MISSION. A SECRET *REPUBLIC* MISSION...
I SEE. I'VE LOST MY COMLINK, BUT IF YOU COULD DIRECT US TO THE PRESIDENTIAL PALACE, I COULD CONSULT WITH SENATOR AMIDALA --
BWEEP!

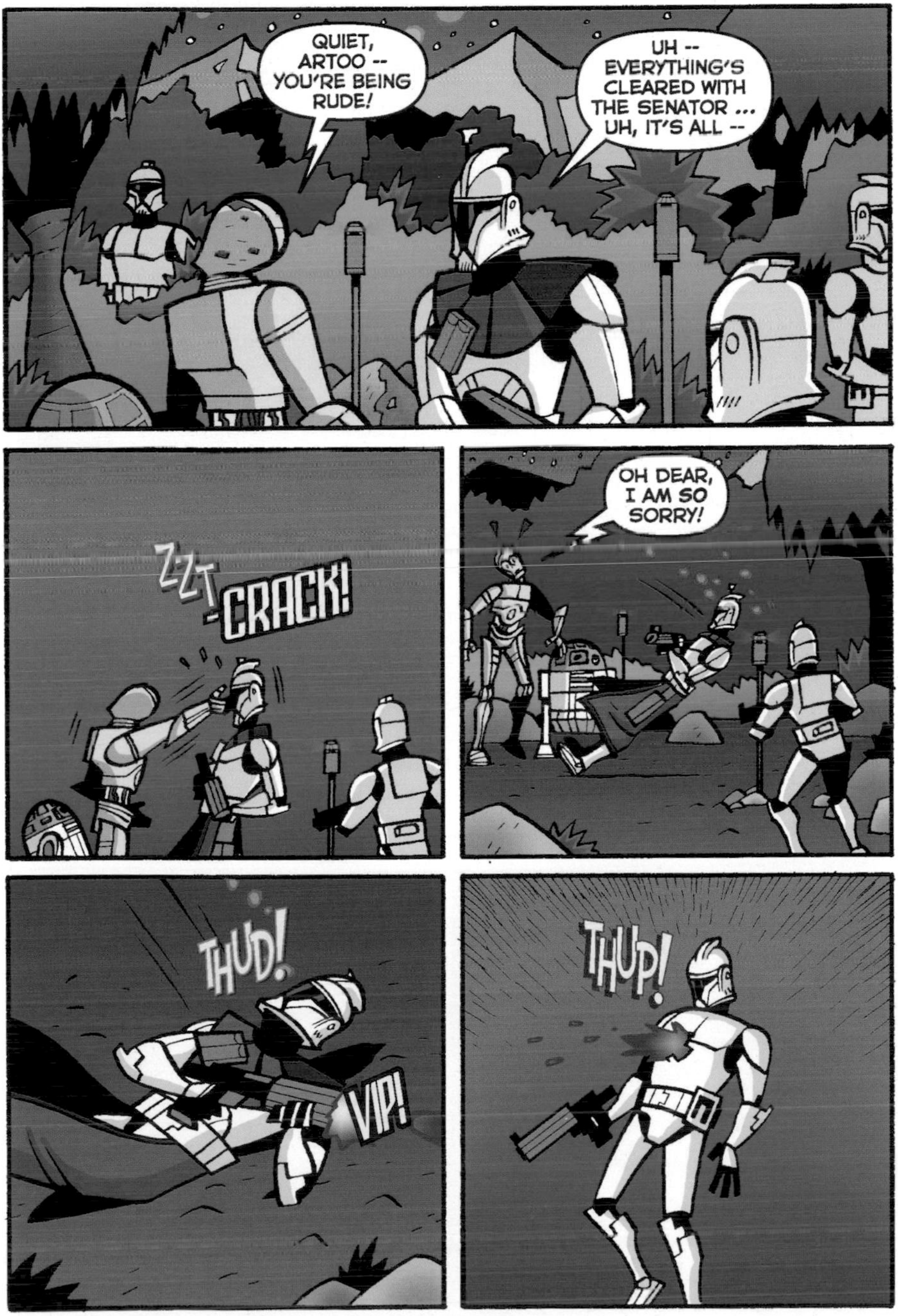
QUIET, ARTOO -- YOU'RE BEING RUDE!
UH -- EVERYTHING'S CLEARED WITH THE SENATOR ... UH, IT'S ALL --
ZZT-CRACK!
OH DEAR, I AM SO SORRY!
THUD!
VIP!
THUP!

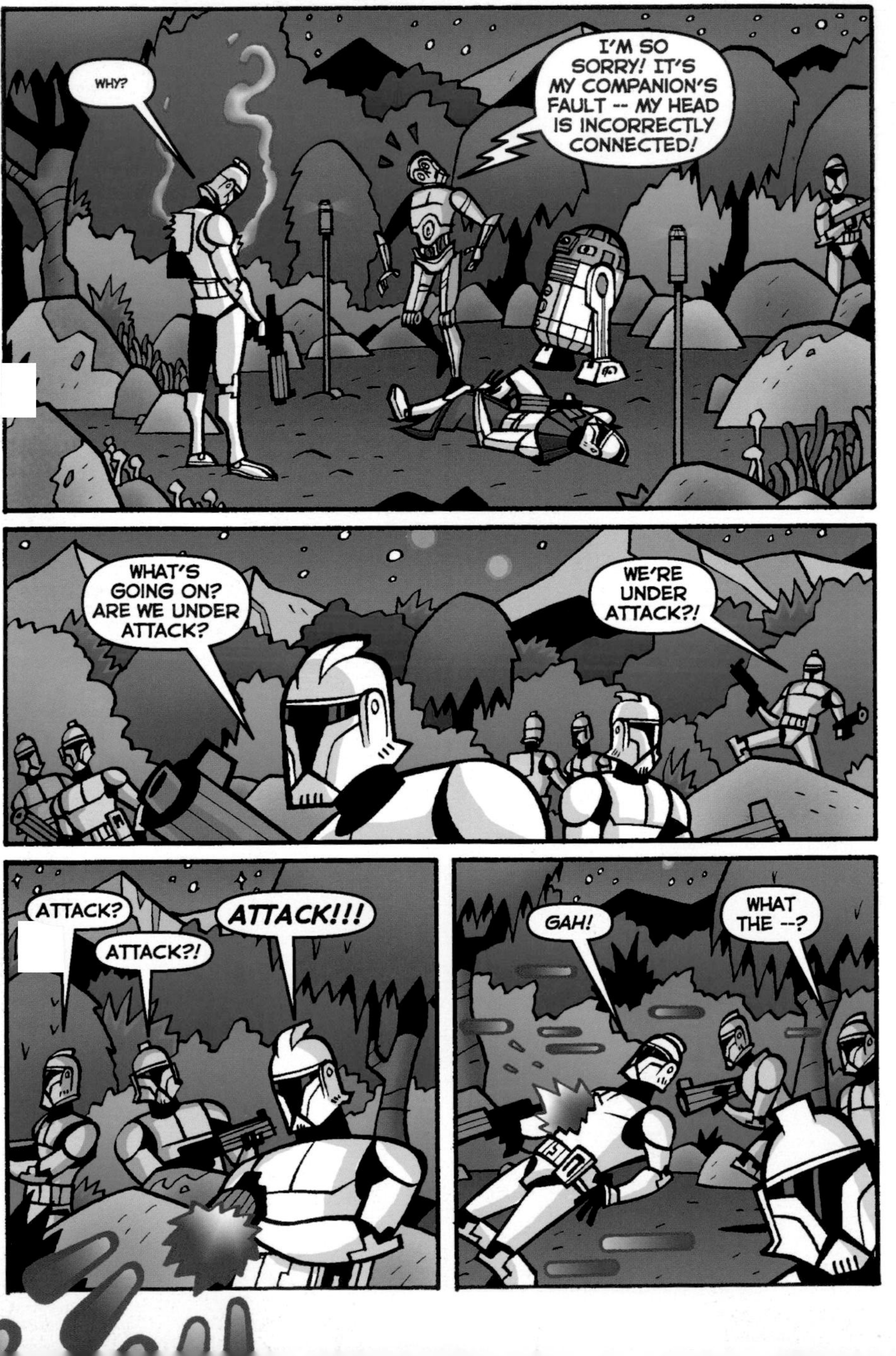
WHY?
I'M SO SORRY! IT'S MY COMPANION'S FAULT -- MY HEAD IS INCORRECTLY CONNECTED!
WHAT'S GOING ON? ARE WE UNDER ATTACK?
WE'RE UNDER ATTACK?!
ATTACK?
ATTACK?!
ATTACK!!!
GAH!
WHAT THE --?

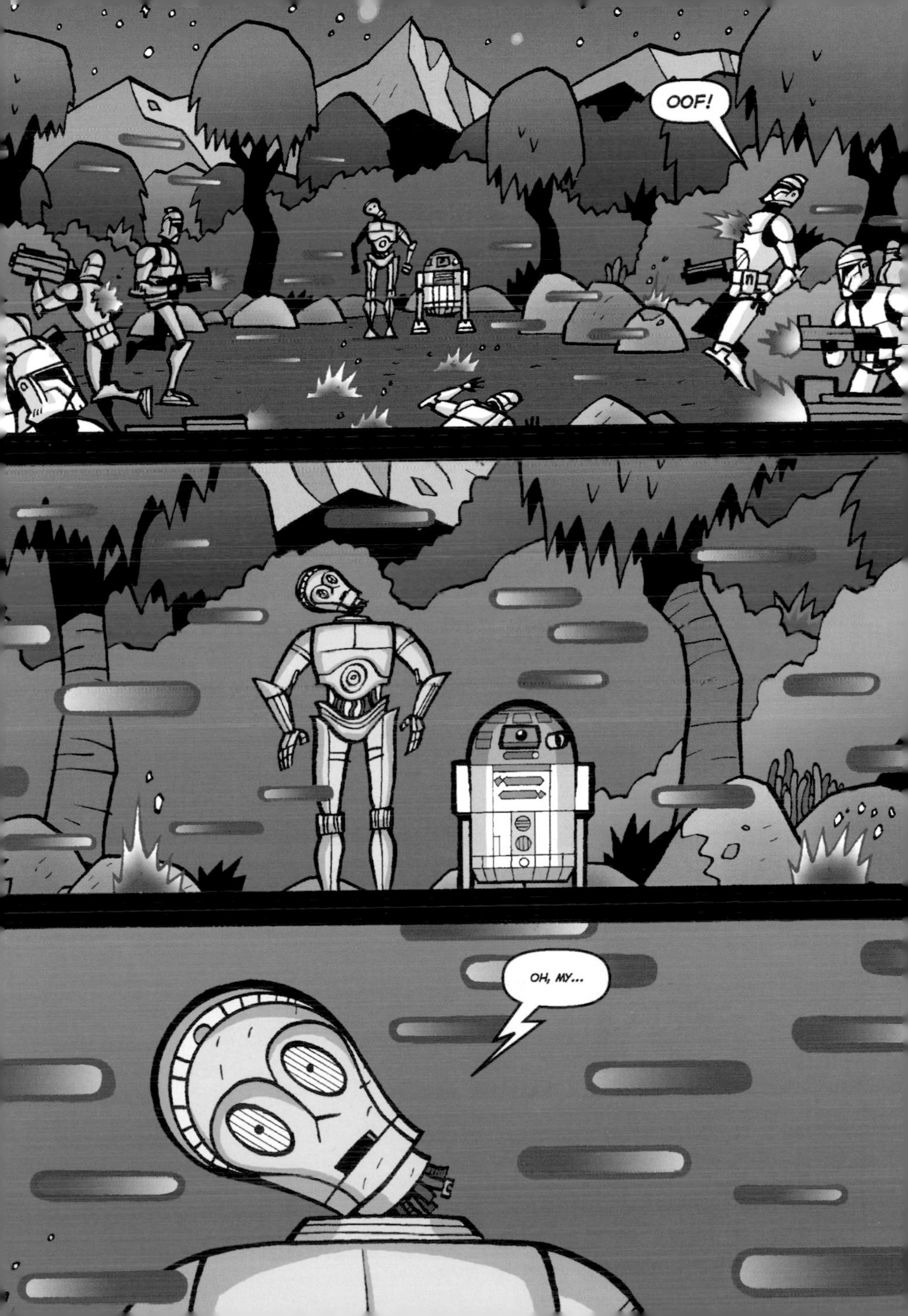
OOF!
OH, MY...

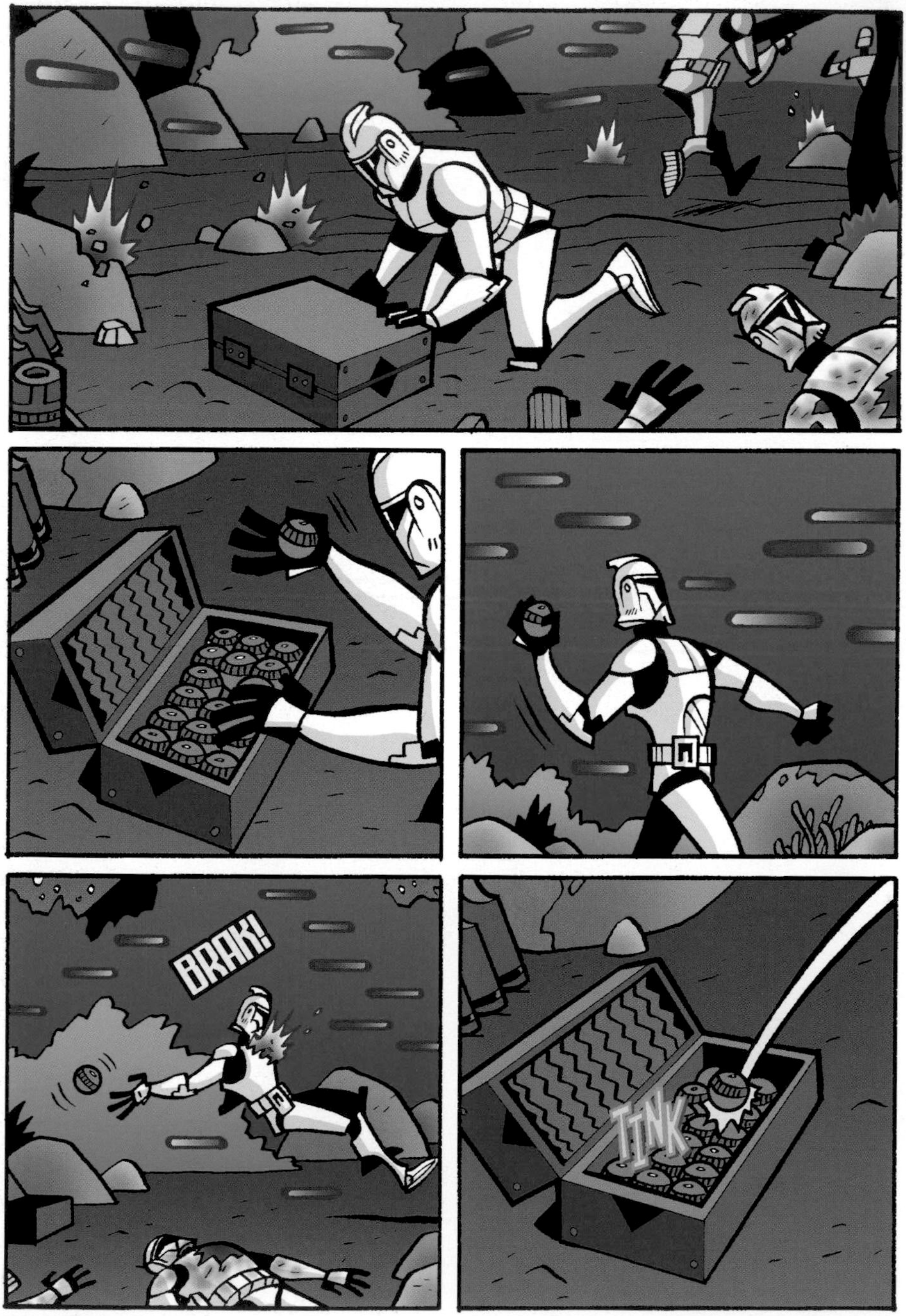
BRAK!
TINK

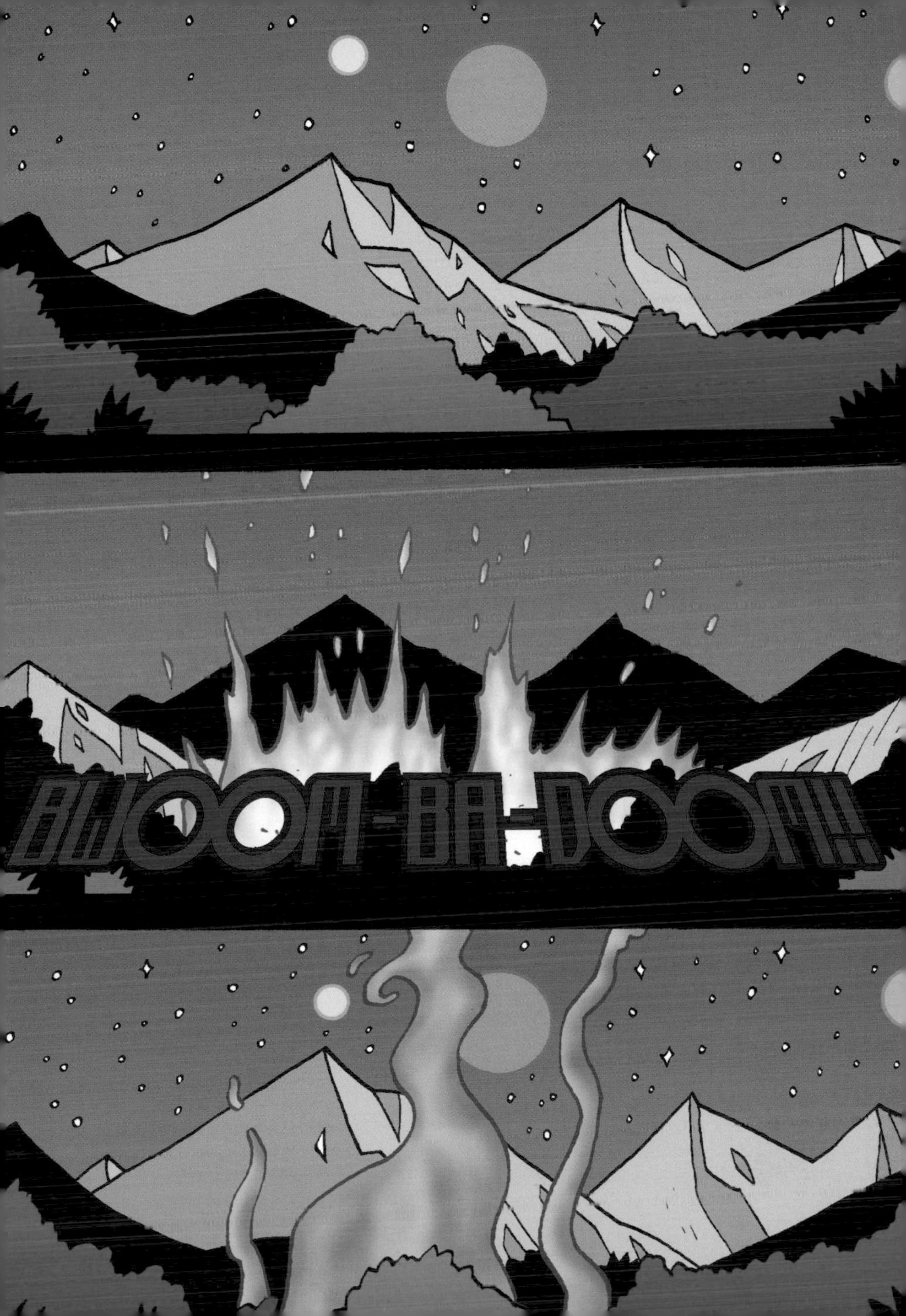
BWOOM-BA-DOOM!!

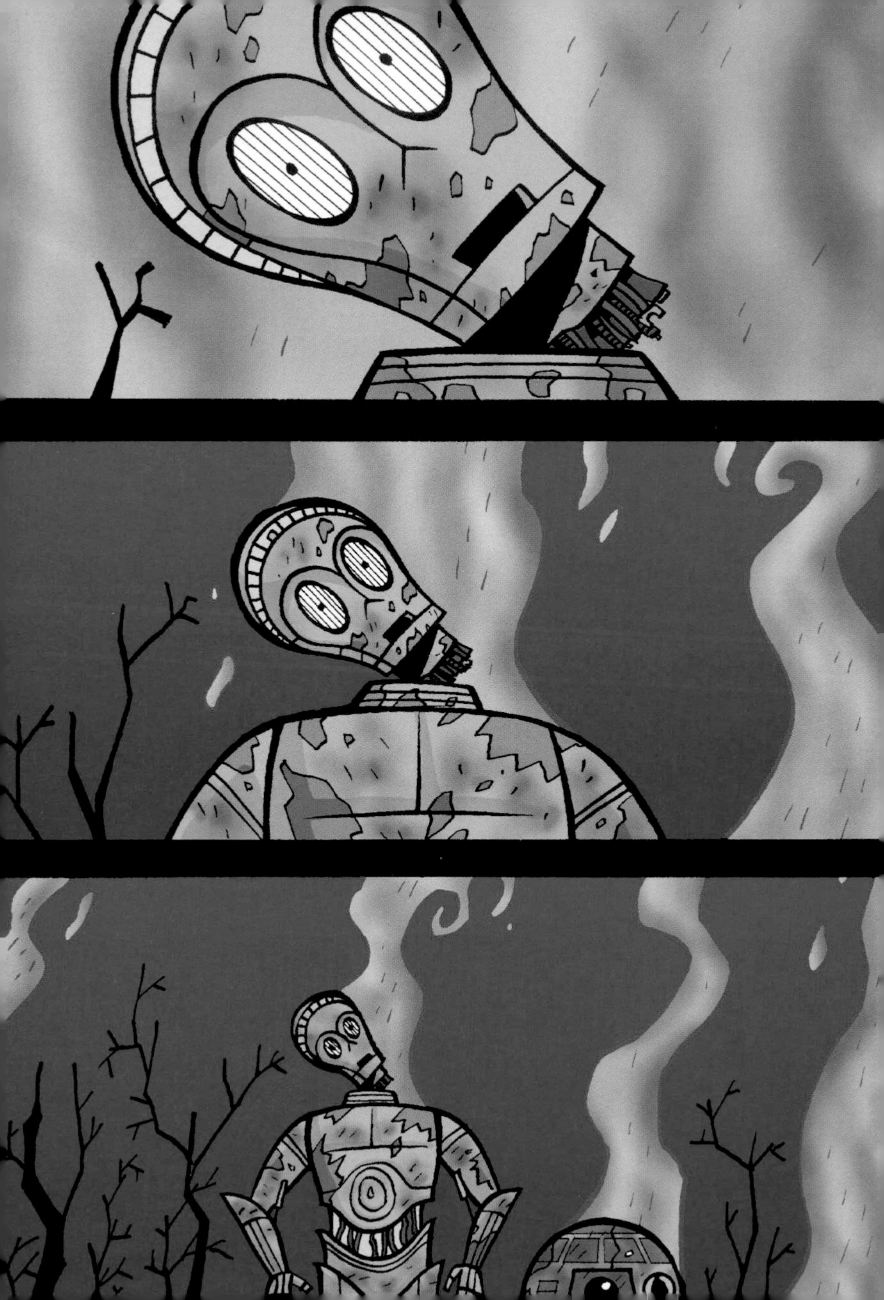

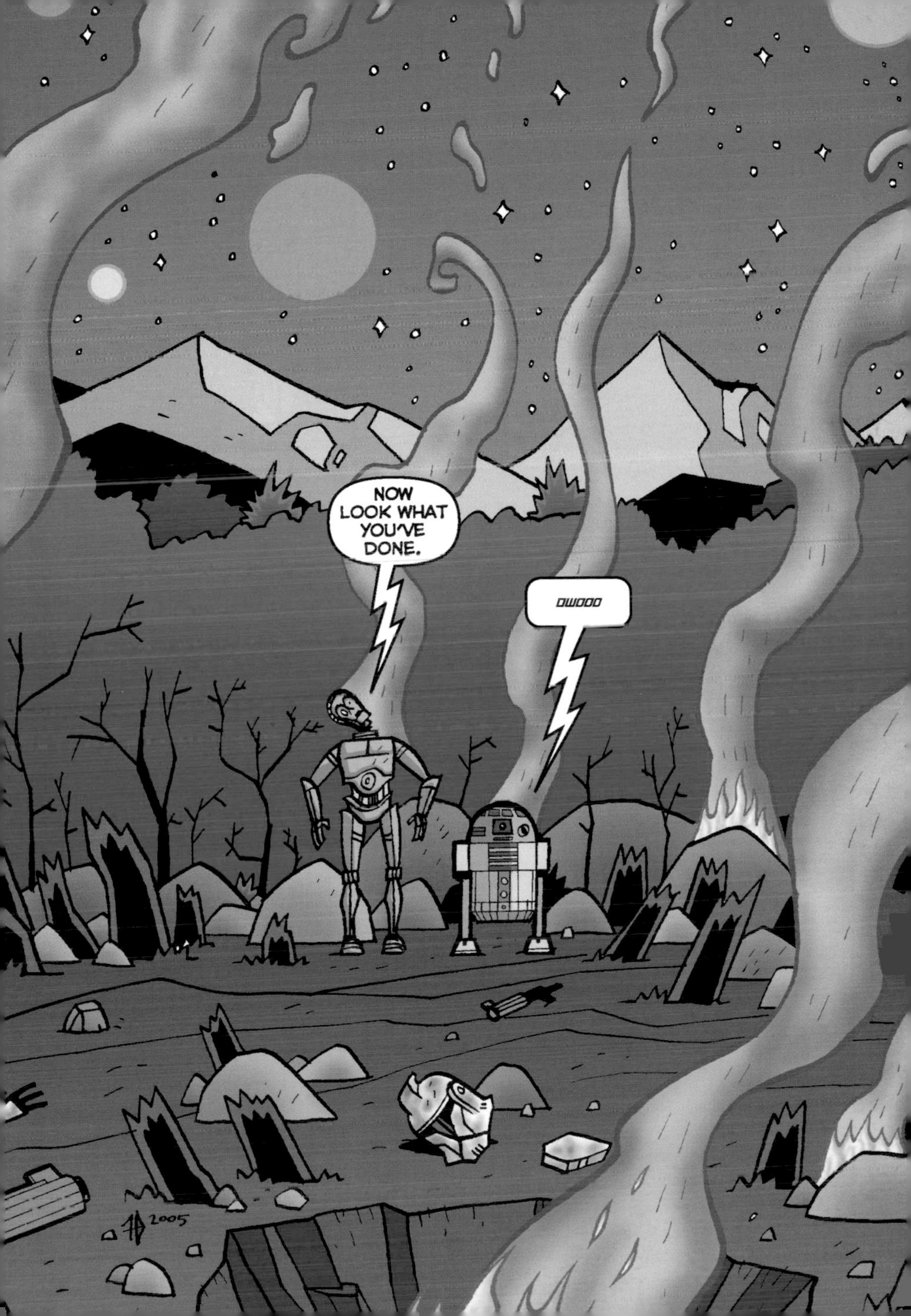
NOW LOOK WHAT YOU'VE DONE.
DWOOO
2005

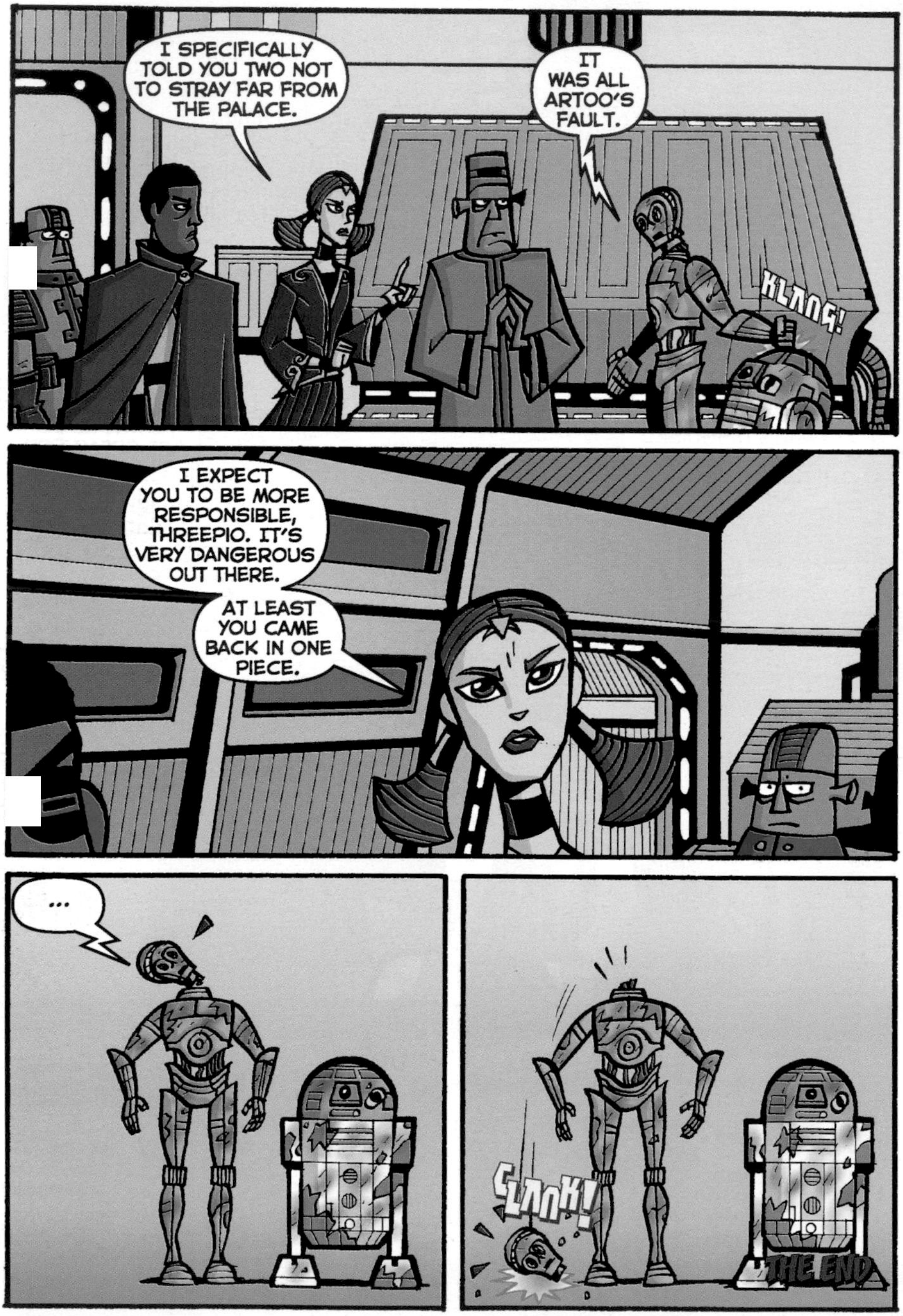
I SPECIFICALLY TOLD YOU TWO NOT TO STRAY FAR FROM THE PALACE.
IT WAS ALL ARTOO'S FAULT.
KLANG!
I EXPECT YOU TO BE MORE RESPONSIBLE, THREEPIO. IT'S VERY DANGEROUS OUT THERE.
AT LEAST YOU CAME BACK IN ONE PIECE.
...
CLANK!
THE END

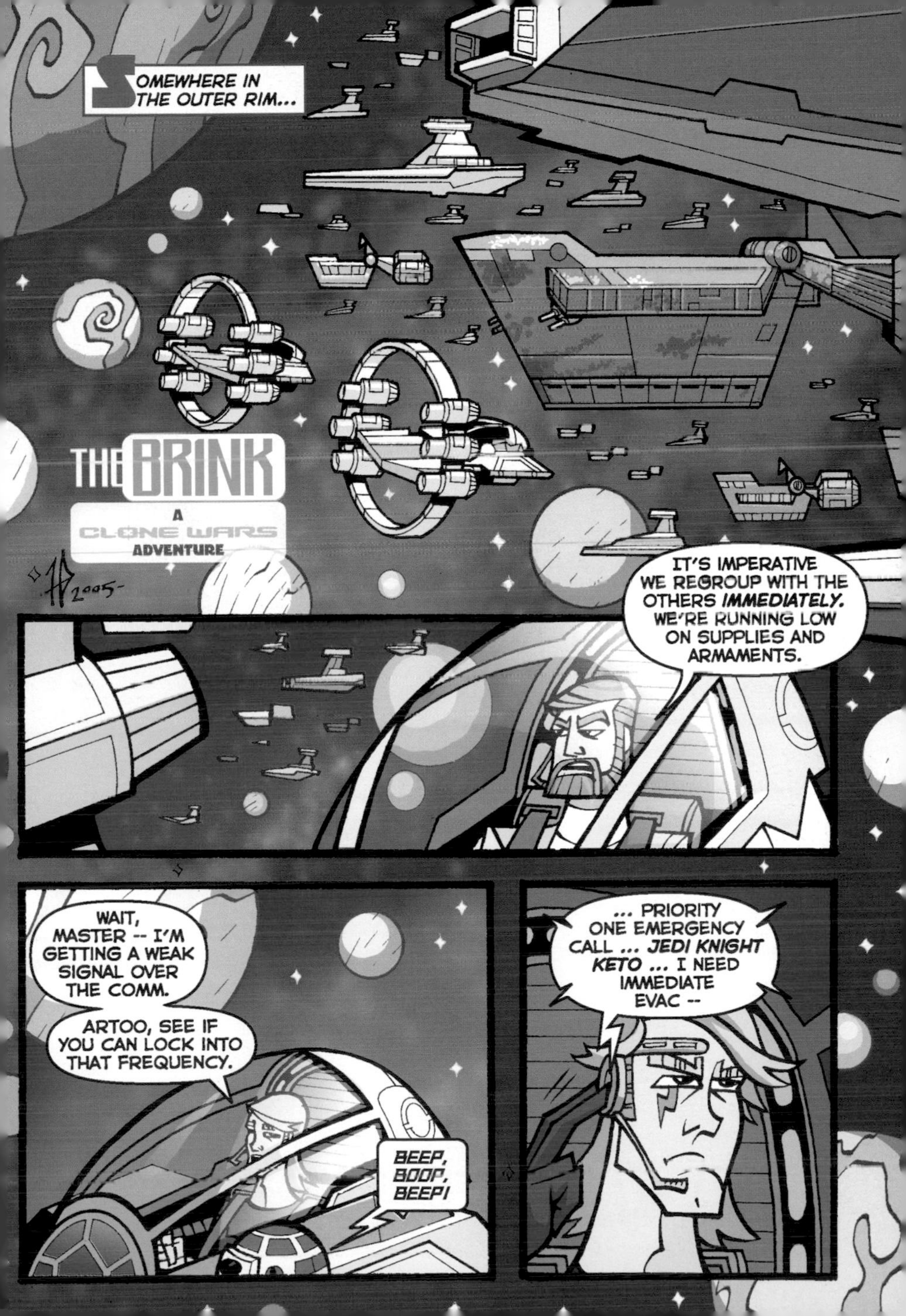
SOMEWHERE IN THE OUTER RIM...
THE BRINK
A CLONE WARS ADVENTURE
IT'S IMPERATIVE WE REGROUP WITH THE OTHERS *IMMEDIATELY.* WE'RE RUNNING LOW ON SUPPLIES AND ARMAMENTS.
WAIT, MASTER -- I'M GETTING A WEAK SIGNAL OVER THE COMM.
ARTOO, SEE IF YOU CAN LOCK INTO THAT FREQUENCY.
BEEP, BOOP, BEEP!
... PRIORITY ONE EMERGENCY CALL ... *JEDI KNIGHT KETO* ... I NEED IMMEDIATE EVAC --

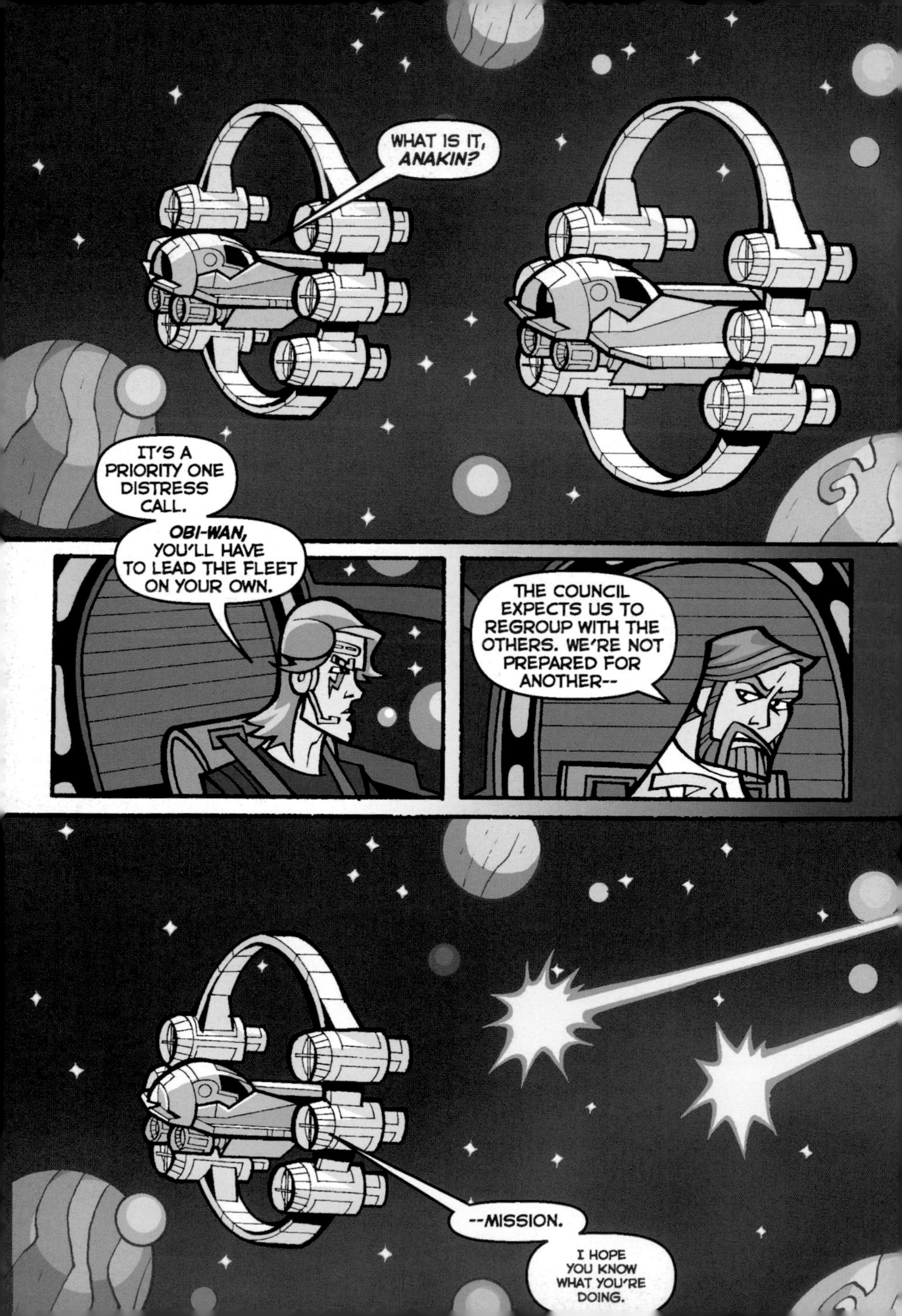
WHAT IS IT, ANAKIN?
IT'S A PRIORITY ONE DISTRESS CALL.
OBI-WAN, YOU'LL HAVE TO LEAD THE FLEET ON YOUR OWN.
THE COUNCIL EXPECTS US TO REGROUP WITH THE OTHERS. WE'RE NOT PREPARED FOR ANOTHER--
--MISSION.
I HOPE YOU KNOW WHAT YOU'RE DOING.

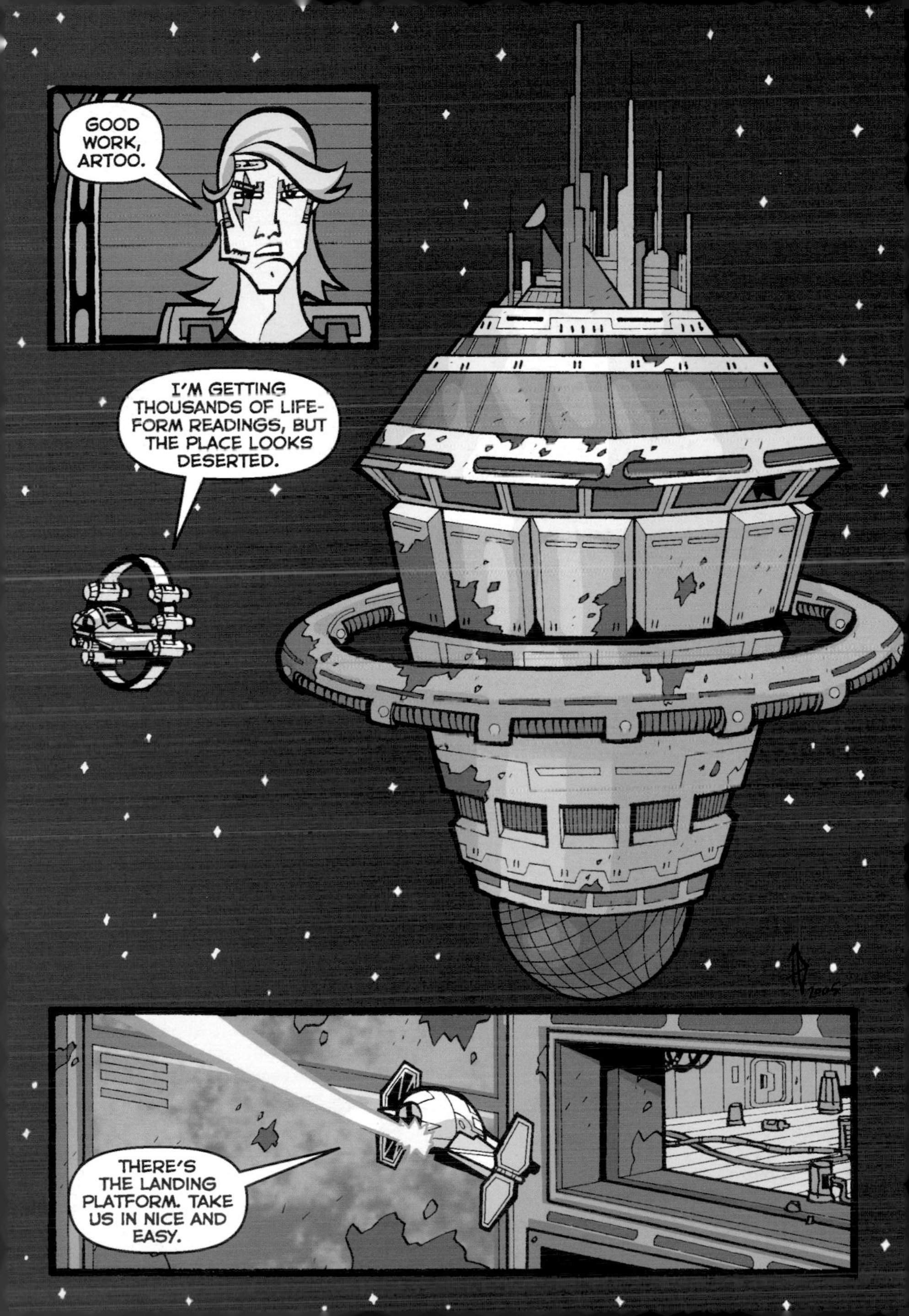
GOOD WORK, ARTOO.
I'M GETTING THOUSANDS OF LIFE-FORM READINGS, BUT THE PLACE LOOKS DESERTED.
THERE'S THE LANDING PLATFORM. TAKE US IN NICE AND EASY.

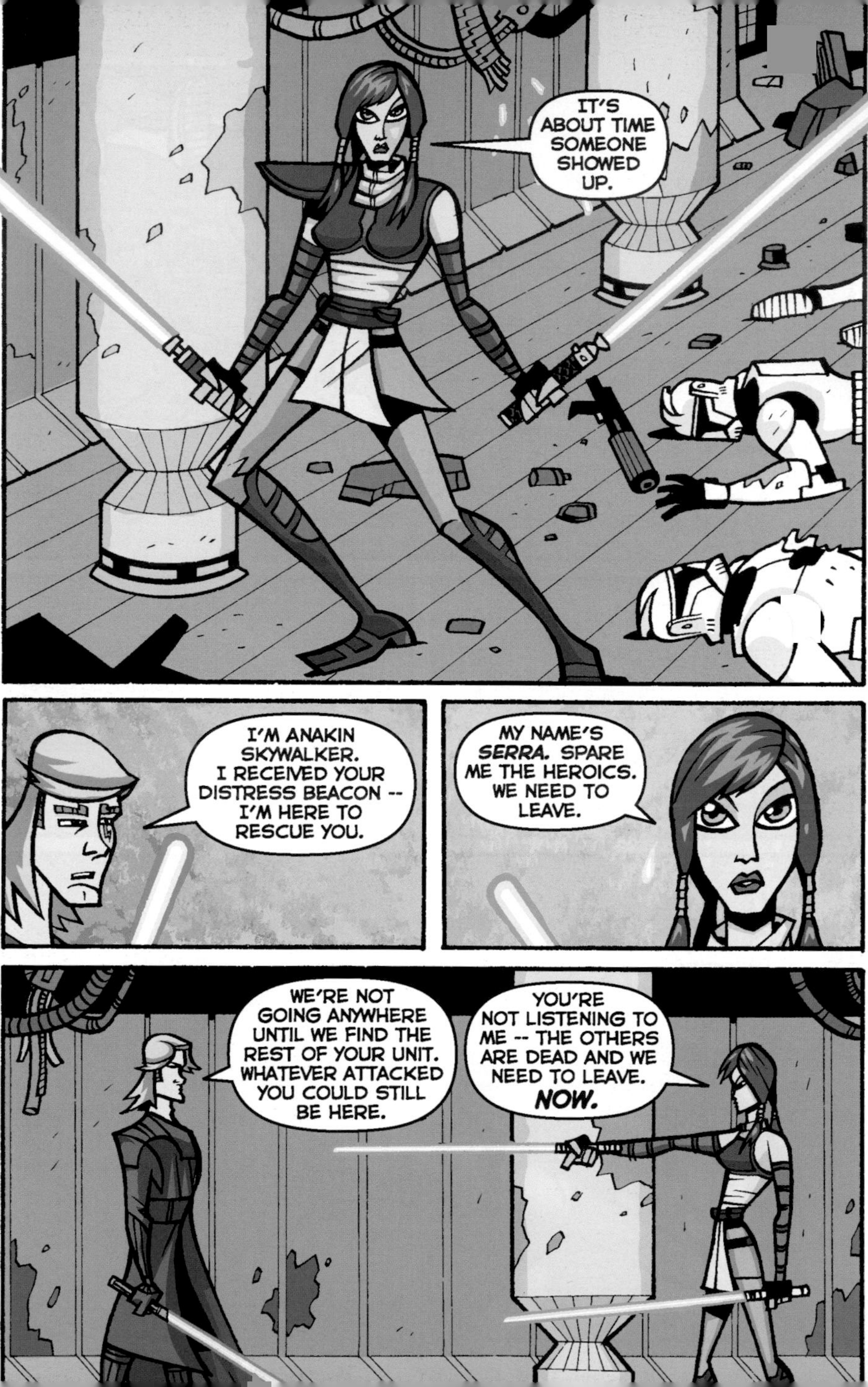
IT'S ABOUT TIME SOMEONE SHOWED UP.
I'M ANAKIN SKYWALKER. I RECEIVED YOUR DISTRESS BEACON -- I'M HERE TO RESCUE YOU.
MY NAME'S *SERRA.* SPARE ME THE HEROICS. WE NEED TO LEAVE.
WE'RE NOT GOING ANYWHERE UNTIL WE FIND THE REST OF YOUR UNIT. WHATEVER ATTACKED YOU COULD STILL BE HERE.
YOU'RE NOT LISTENING TO ME -- THE OTHERS ARE DEAD AND WE NEED TO LEAVE. ***NOW.***

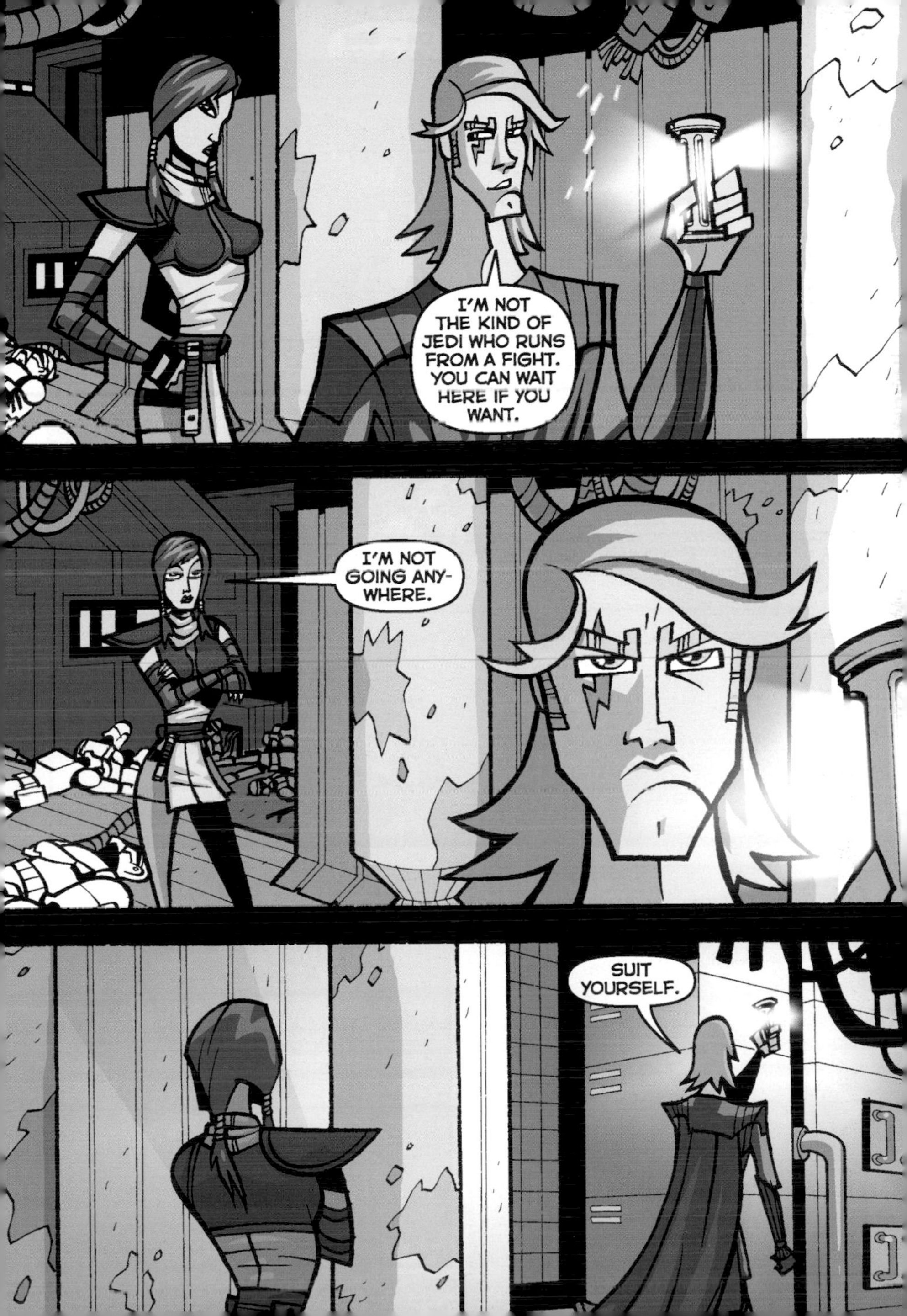
I'M NOT THE KIND OF JEDI WHO RUNS FROM A FIGHT. YOU CAN WAIT HERE IF YOU WANT.
I'M NOT GOING ANY-WHERE.
SUIT YOURSELF.

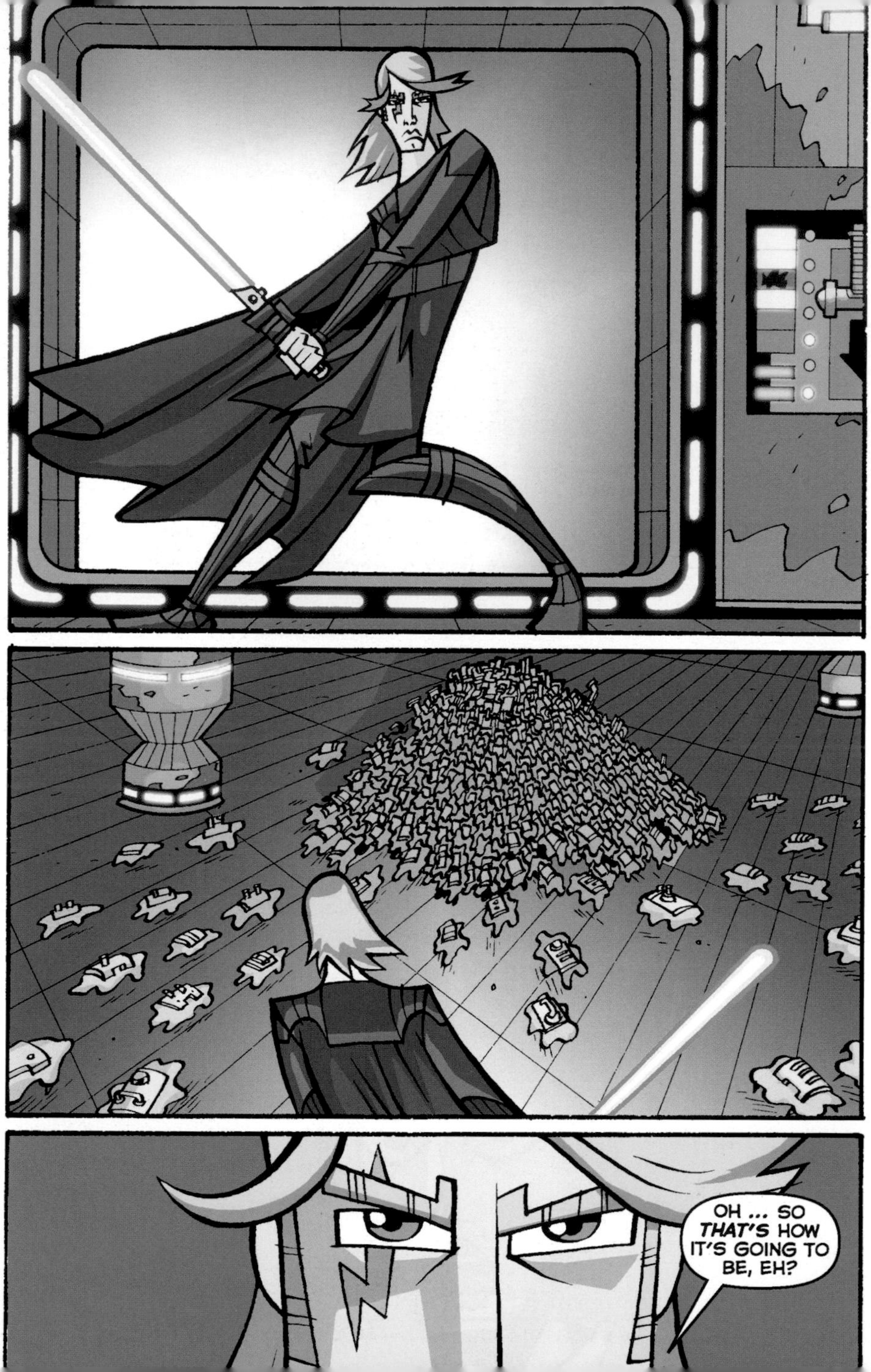
OH ... SO *THAT'S* HOW IT'S GOING TO BE, EH?

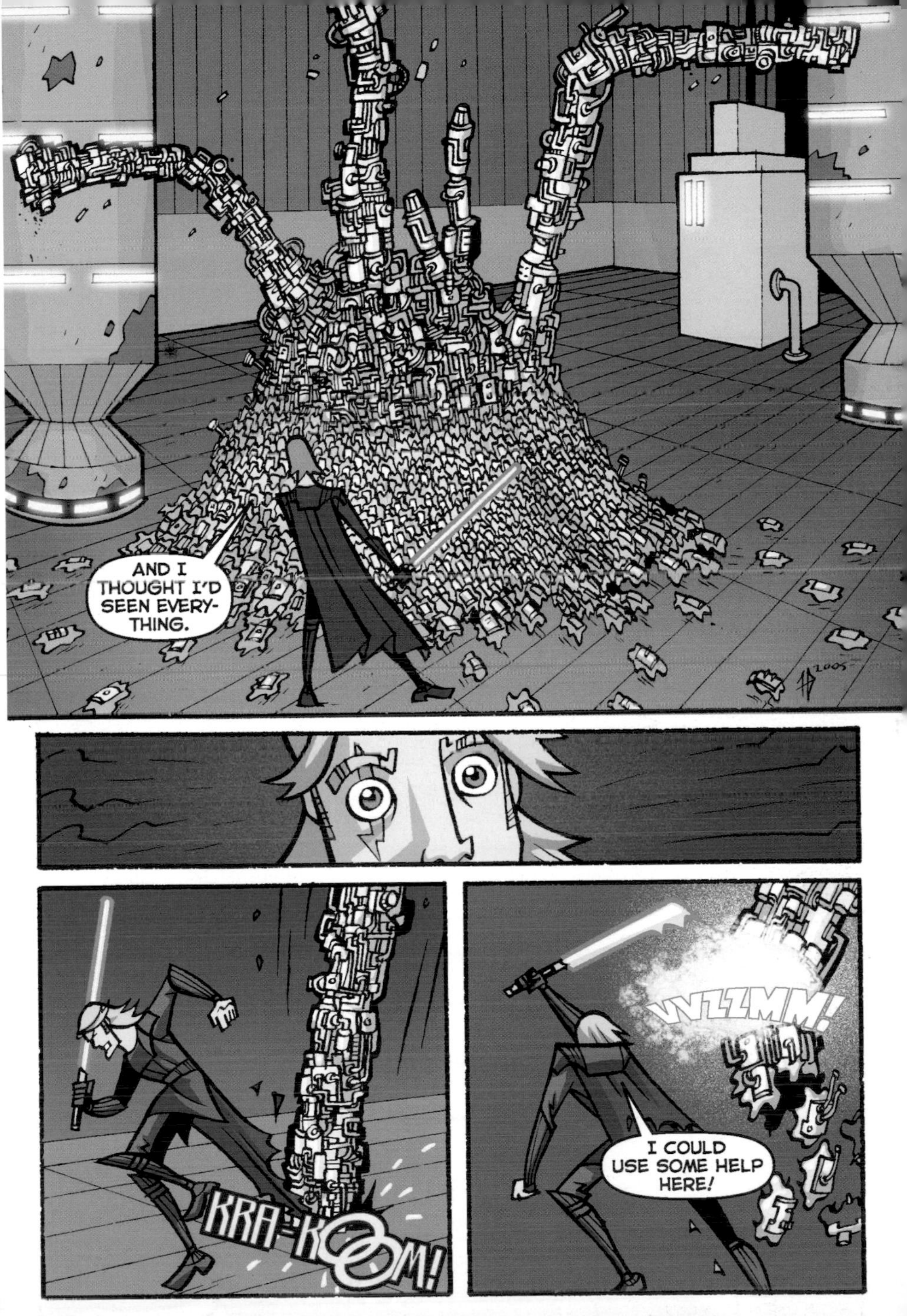
AND I THOUGHT I'D SEEN EVERY-THING.
KRA-KOOM!
VVZZMM!
I COULD USE SOME HELP HERE!

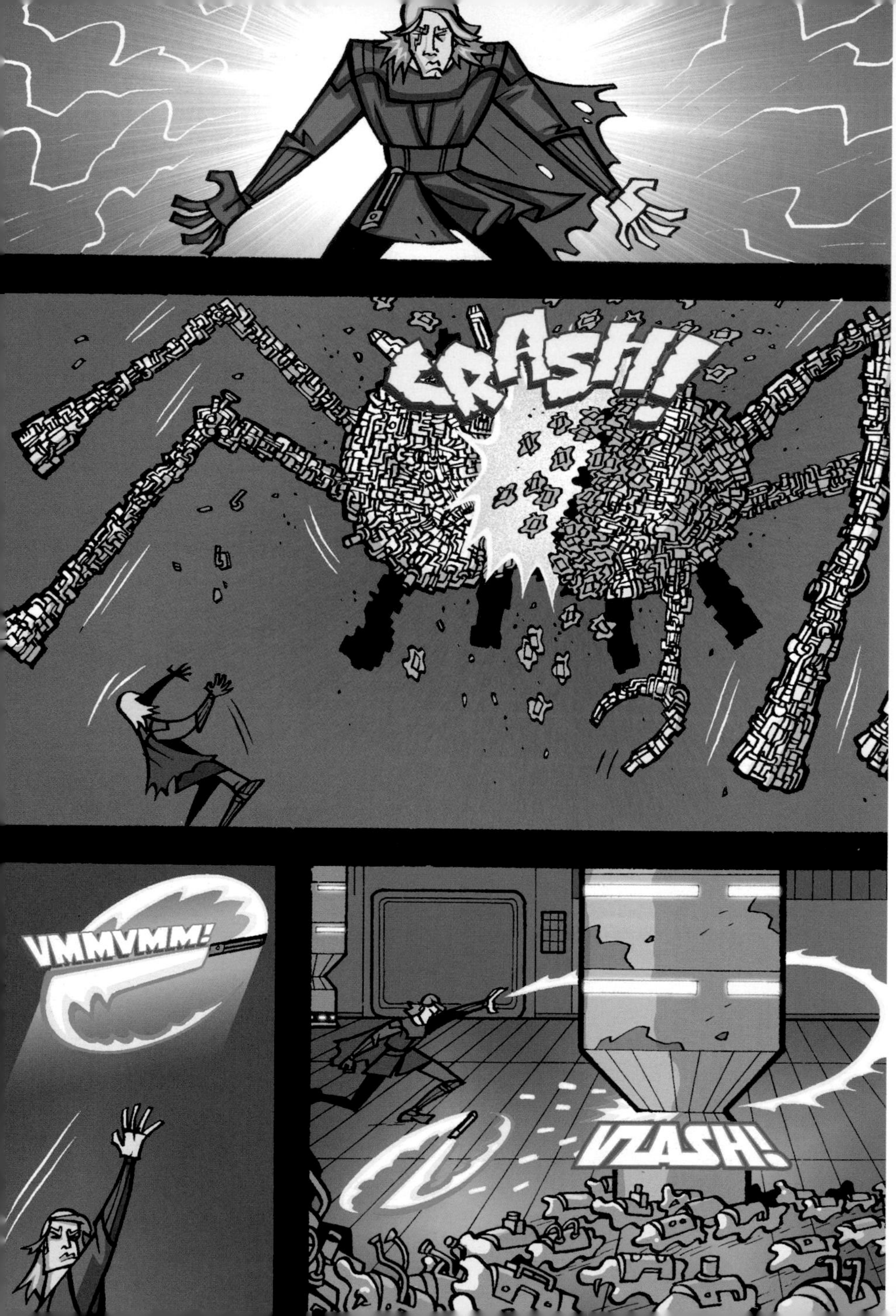
CRASH!
VMMVMM!
VZASH!

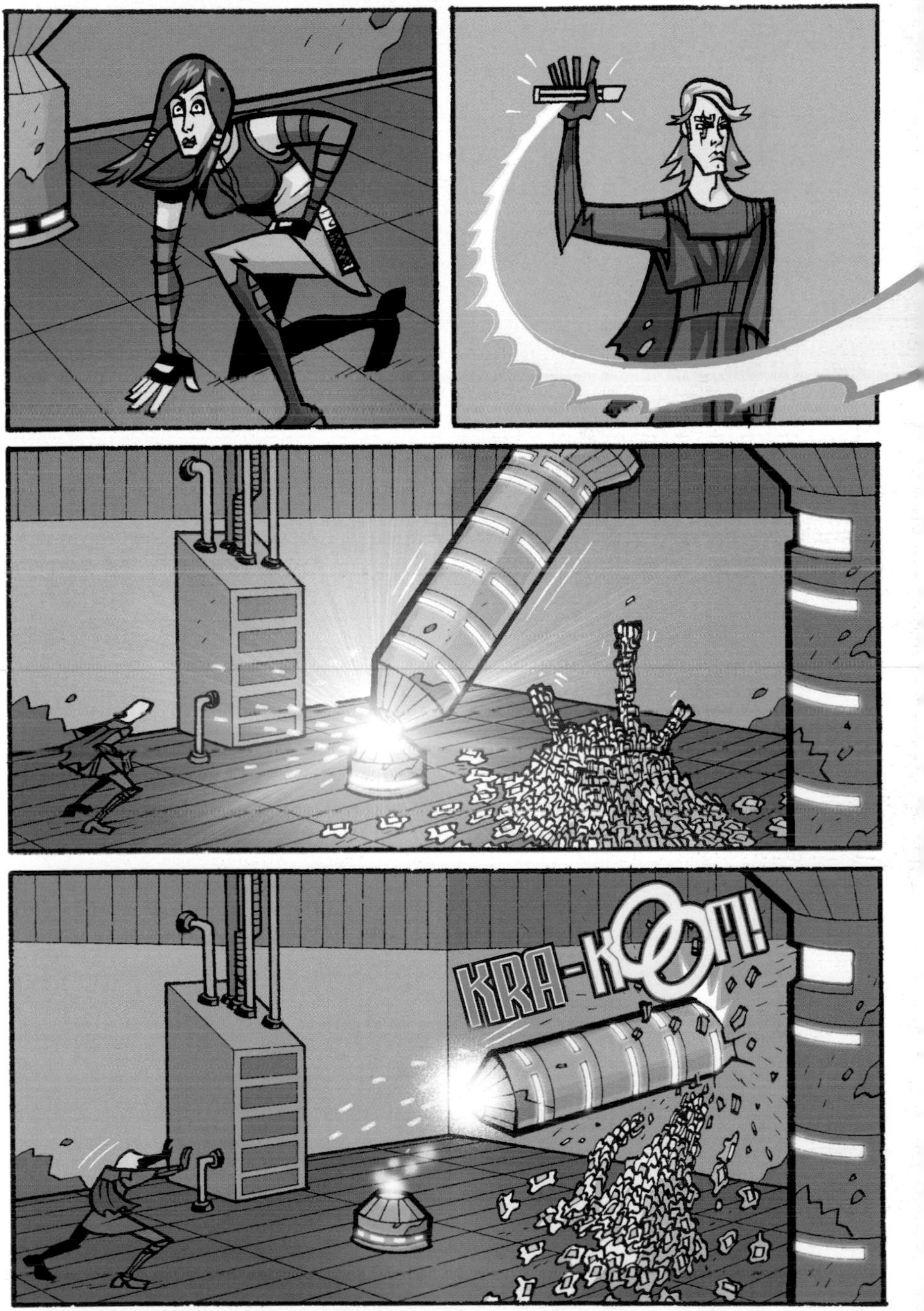
KRA-KOOM!

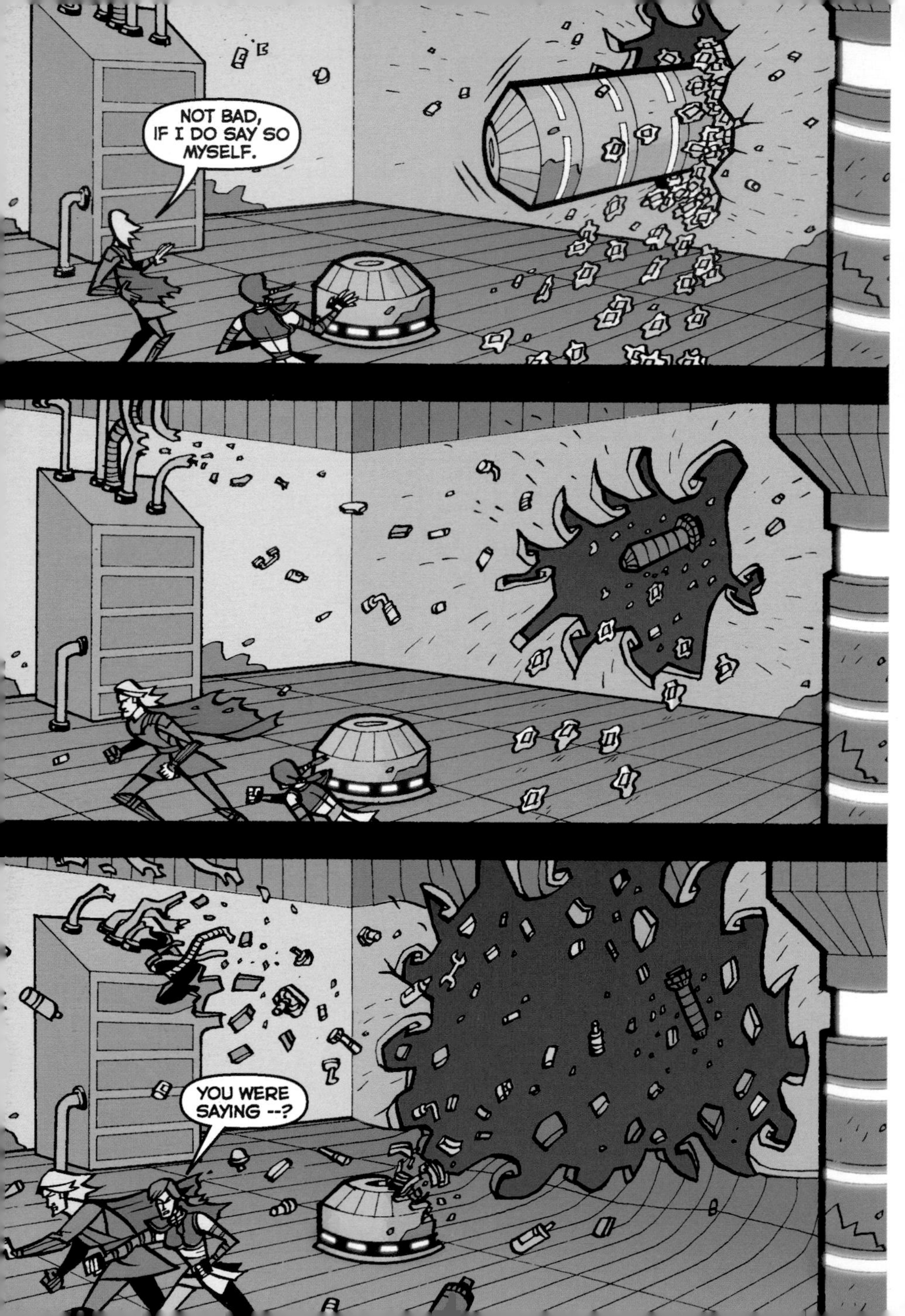
NOT BAD, IF I DO SAY SO MYSELF.
YOU WERE SAYING --?

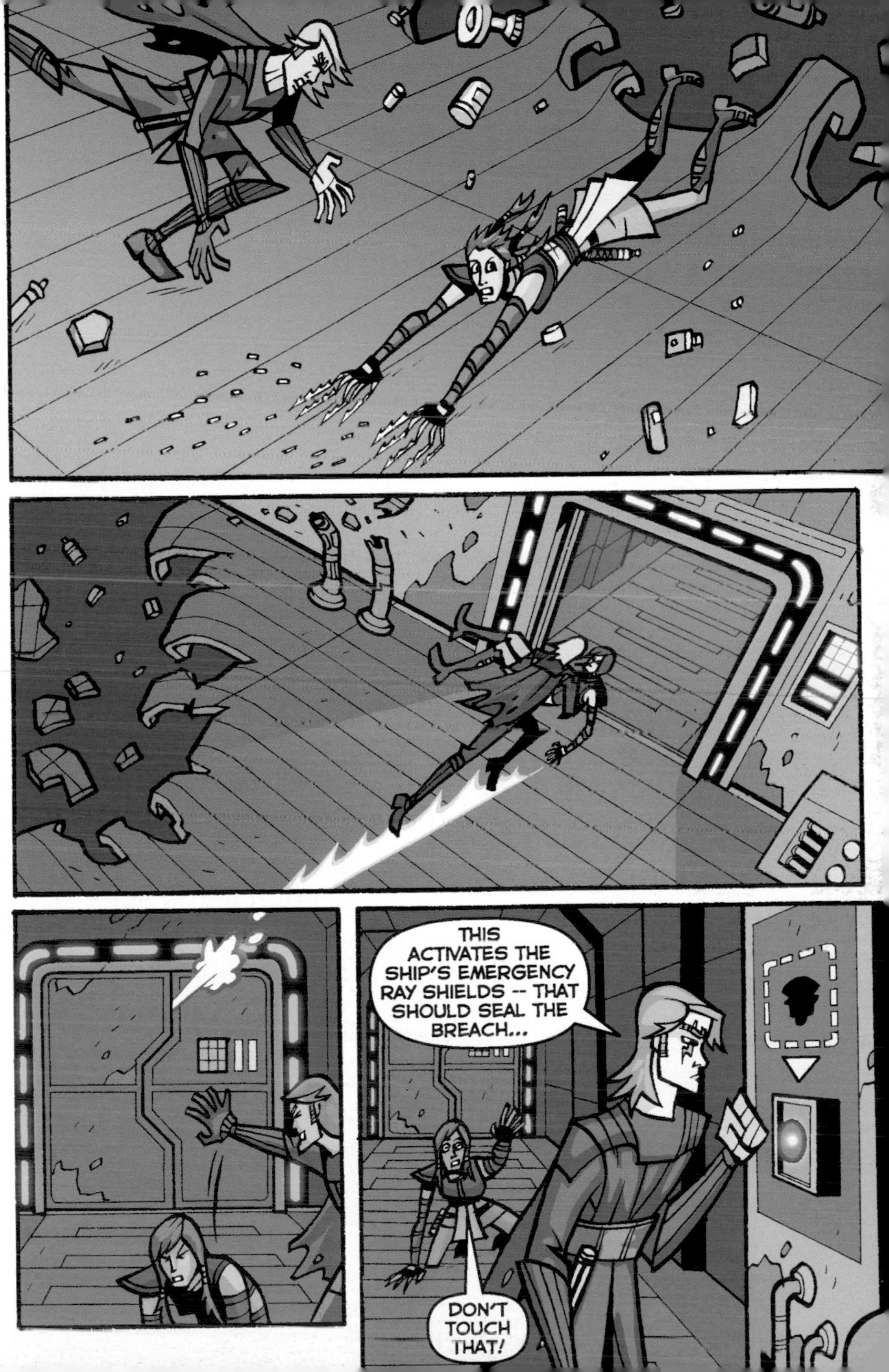
THIS ACTIVATES THE SHIP'S EMERGENCY RAY SHIELDS -- THAT SHOULD SEAL THE BREACH...
DON'T TOUCH THAT!

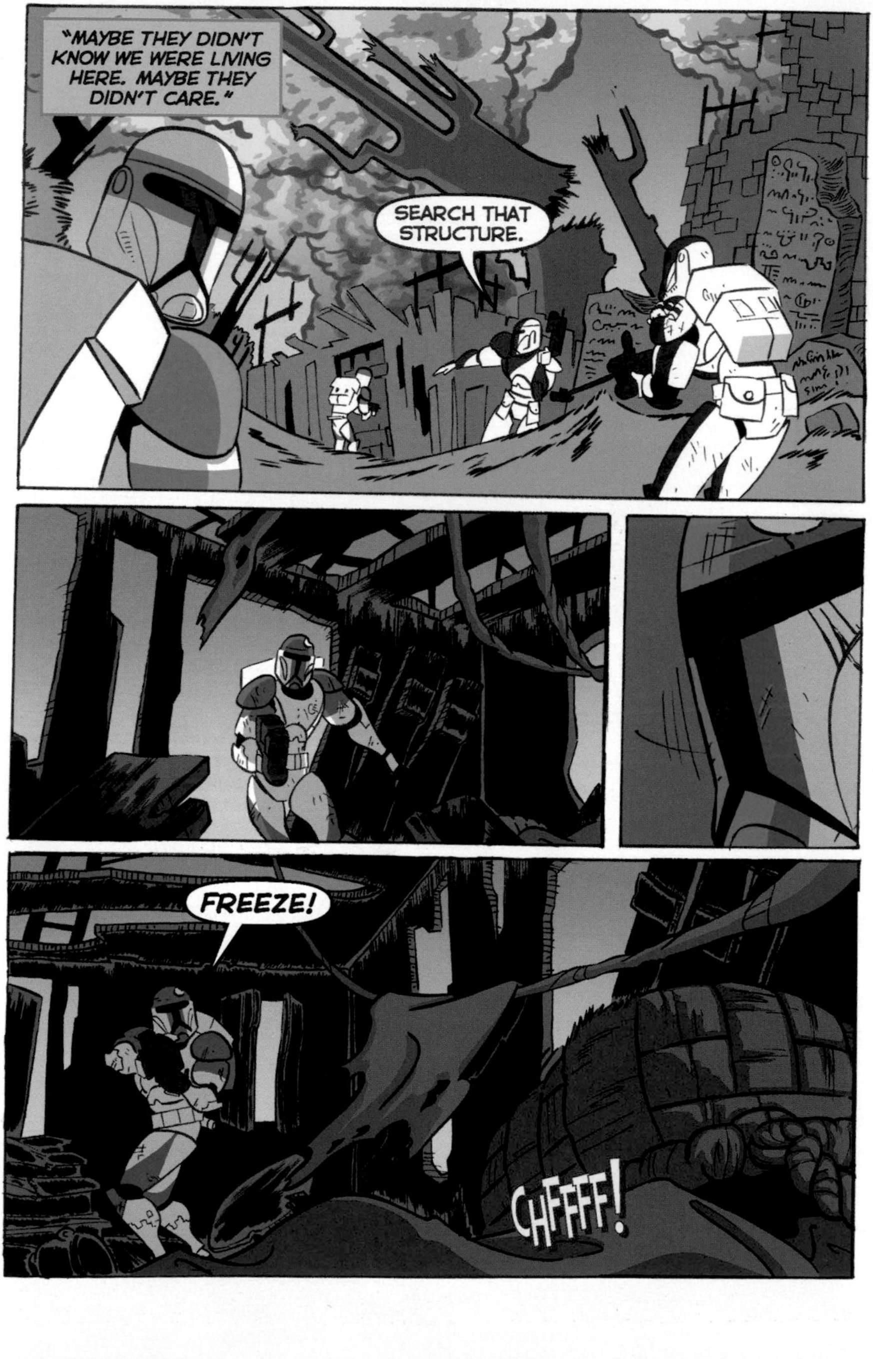
"MAYBE THEY DIDN'T KNOW WE WERE LIVING HERE. MAYBE THEY DIDN'T CARE."
SEARCH THAT STRUCTURE.
FREEZE!
CHFFFF!

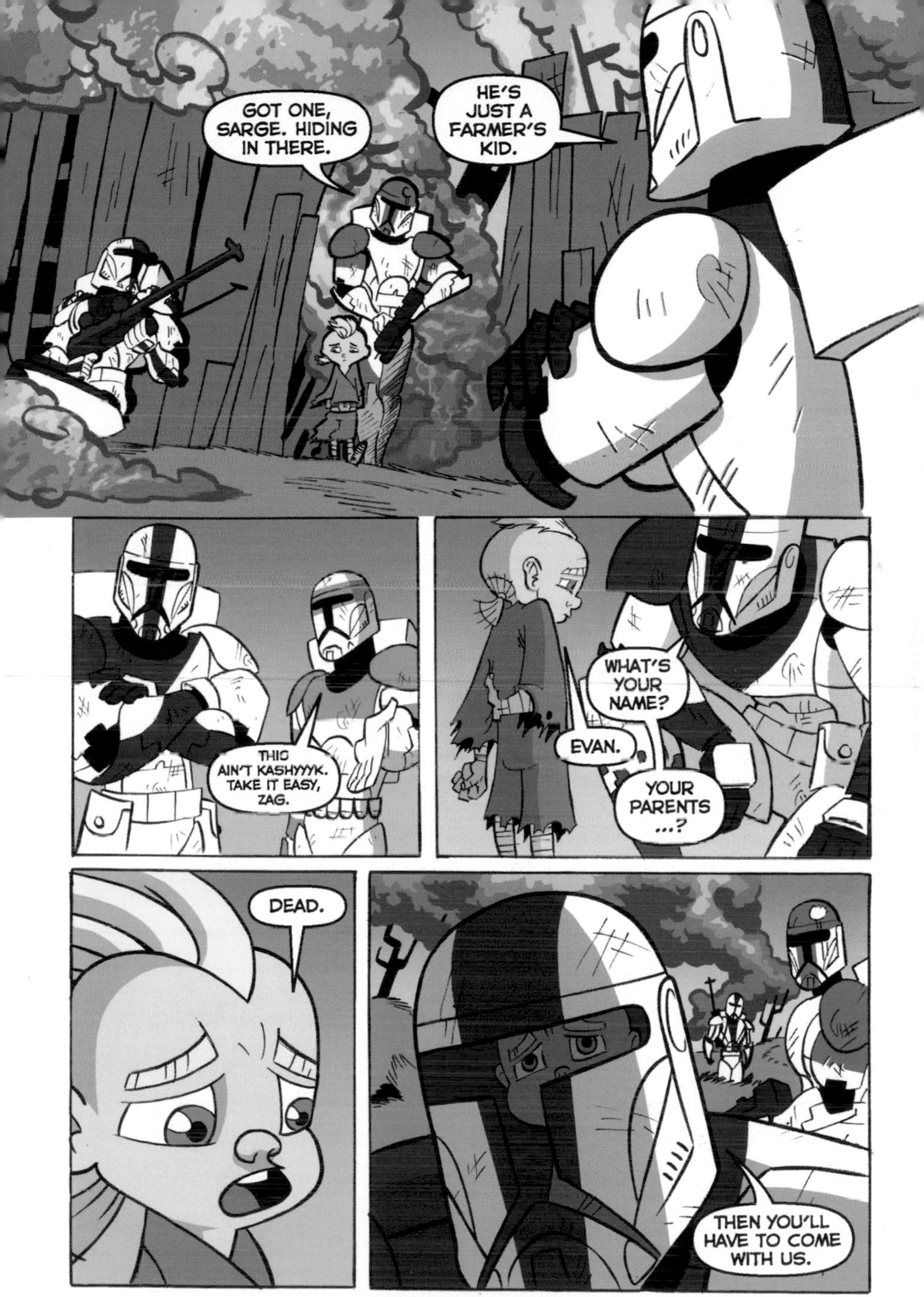

GOT ONE, SARGE. HIDING IN THERE.
HE'S JUST A FARMER'S KID.
THIS AIN'T KASHYYYK. TAKE IT EASY, ZAG.
WHAT'S YOUR NAME?
EVAN.
YOUR PARENTS ...?
DEAD.
THEN YOU'LL HAVE TO COME WITH US.

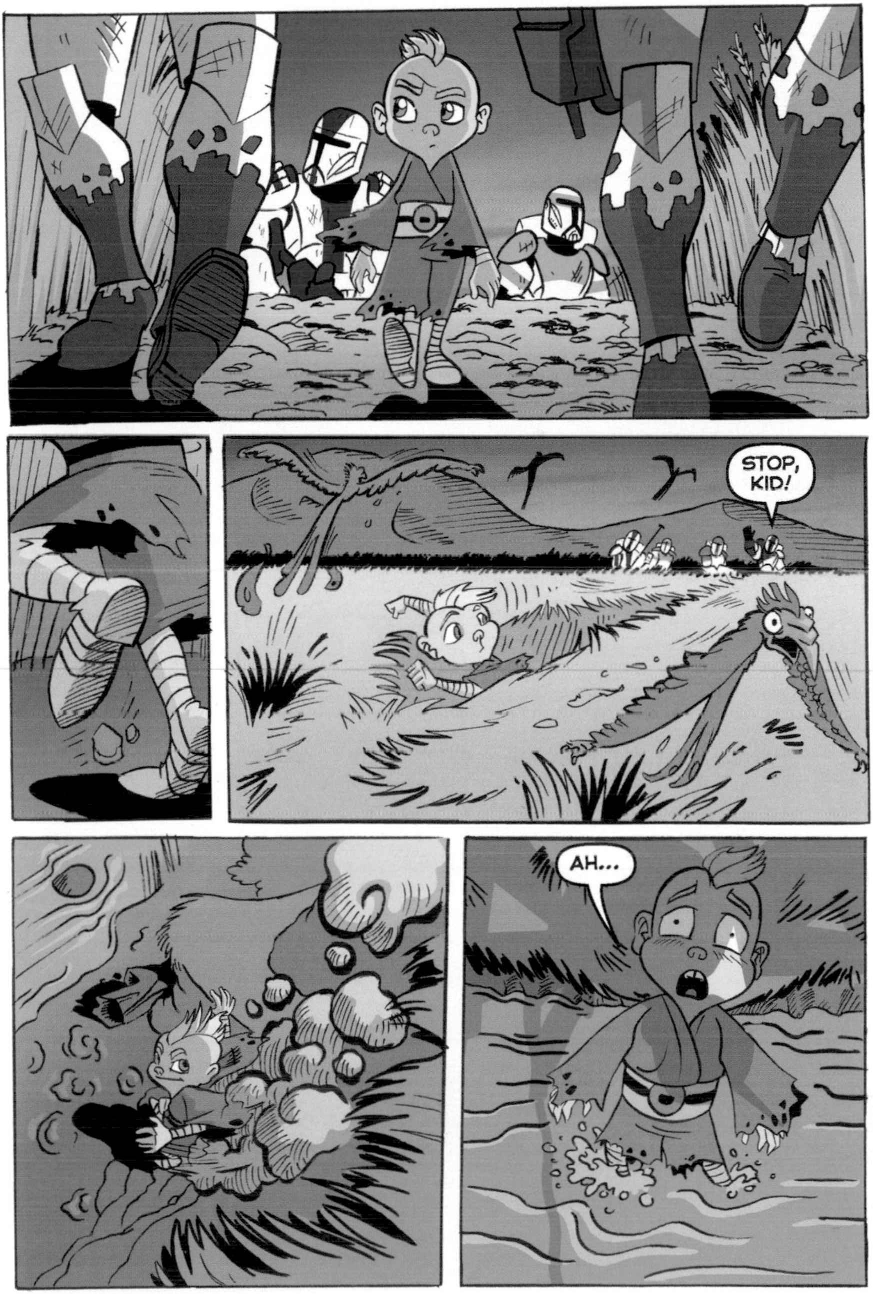
STOP, KID!
AH...

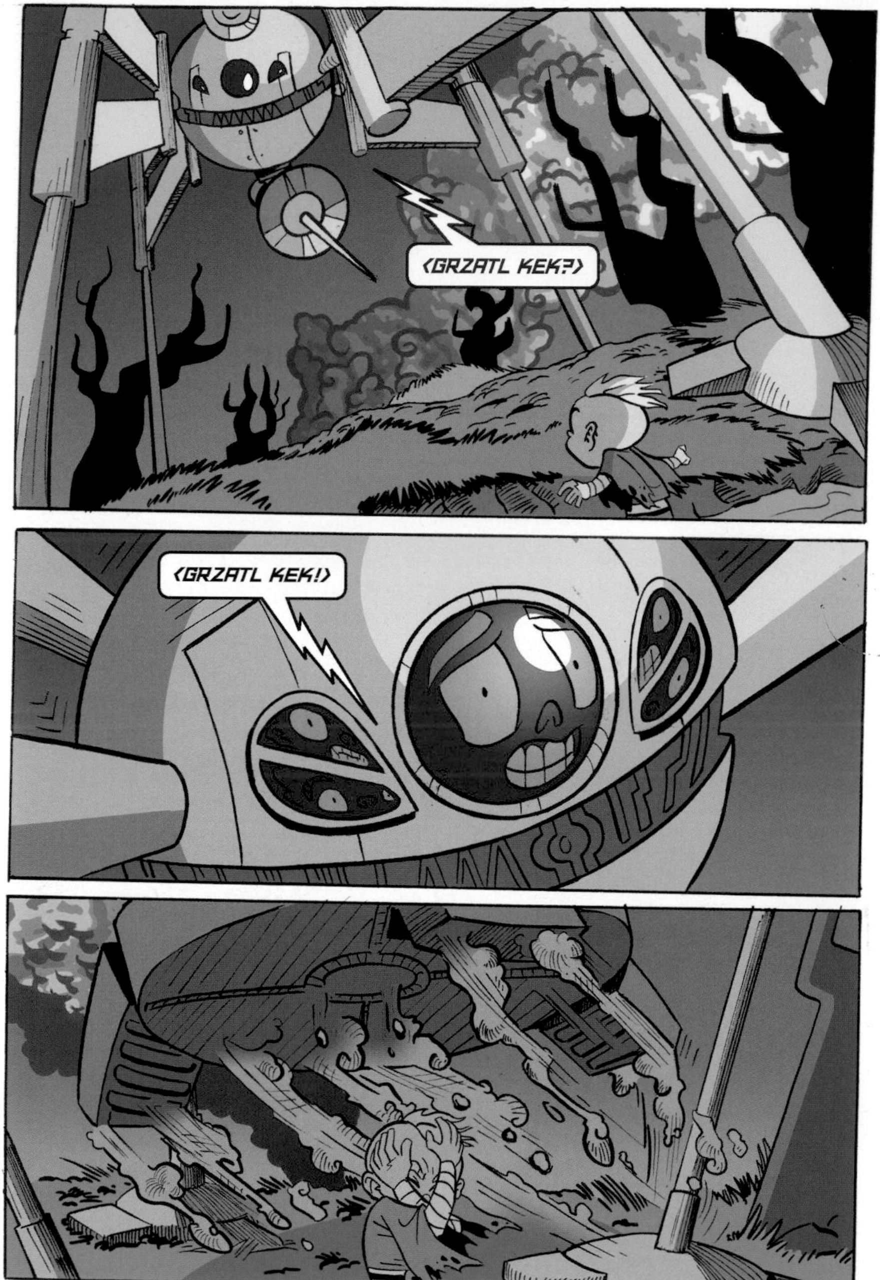
<GRZATL KEK?>
<GRZATL KEK!>

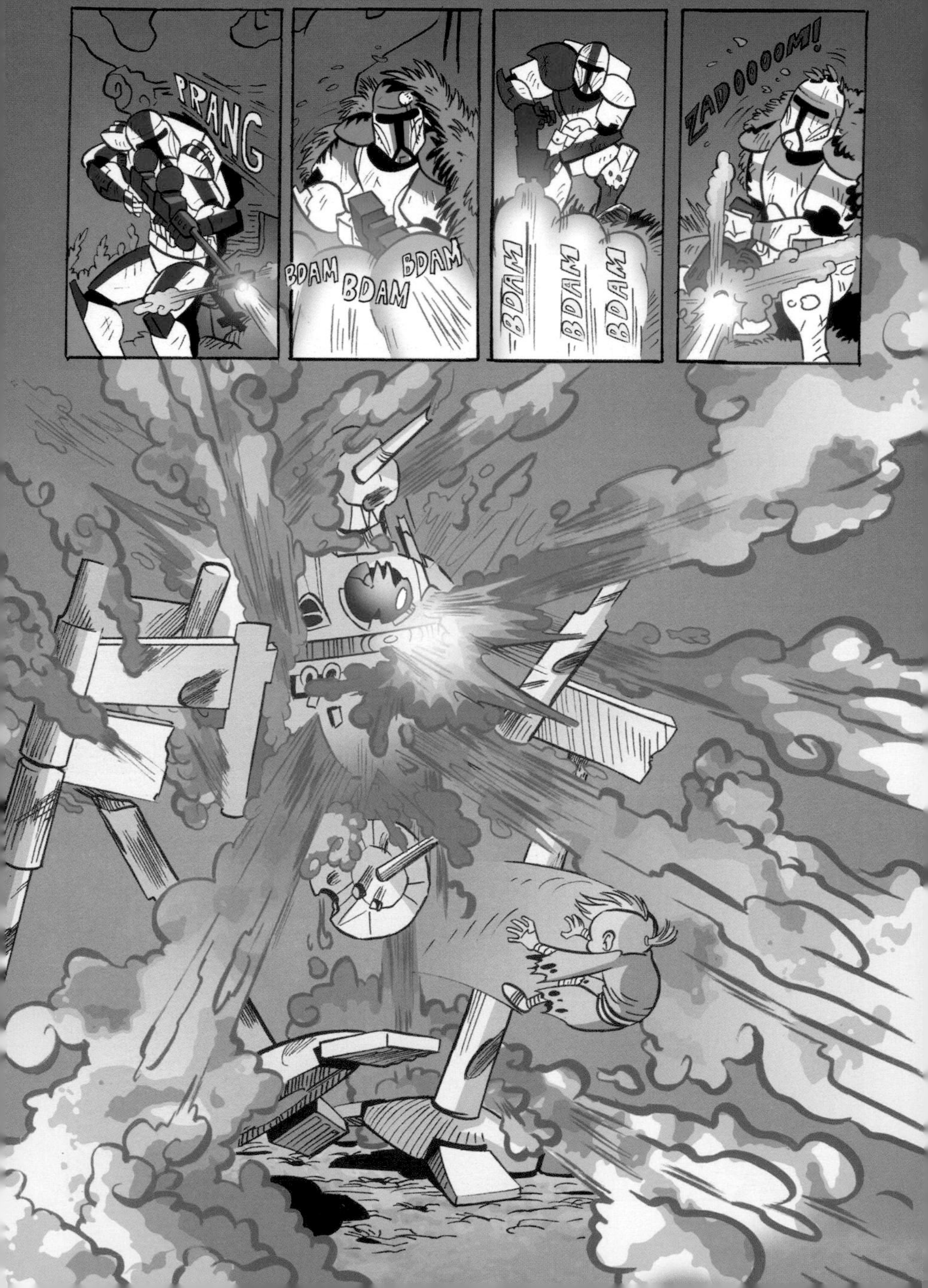
PRANG
BDAM BDAM BDAM
BDAM BDAM BDAM
ZADOOOOOM!

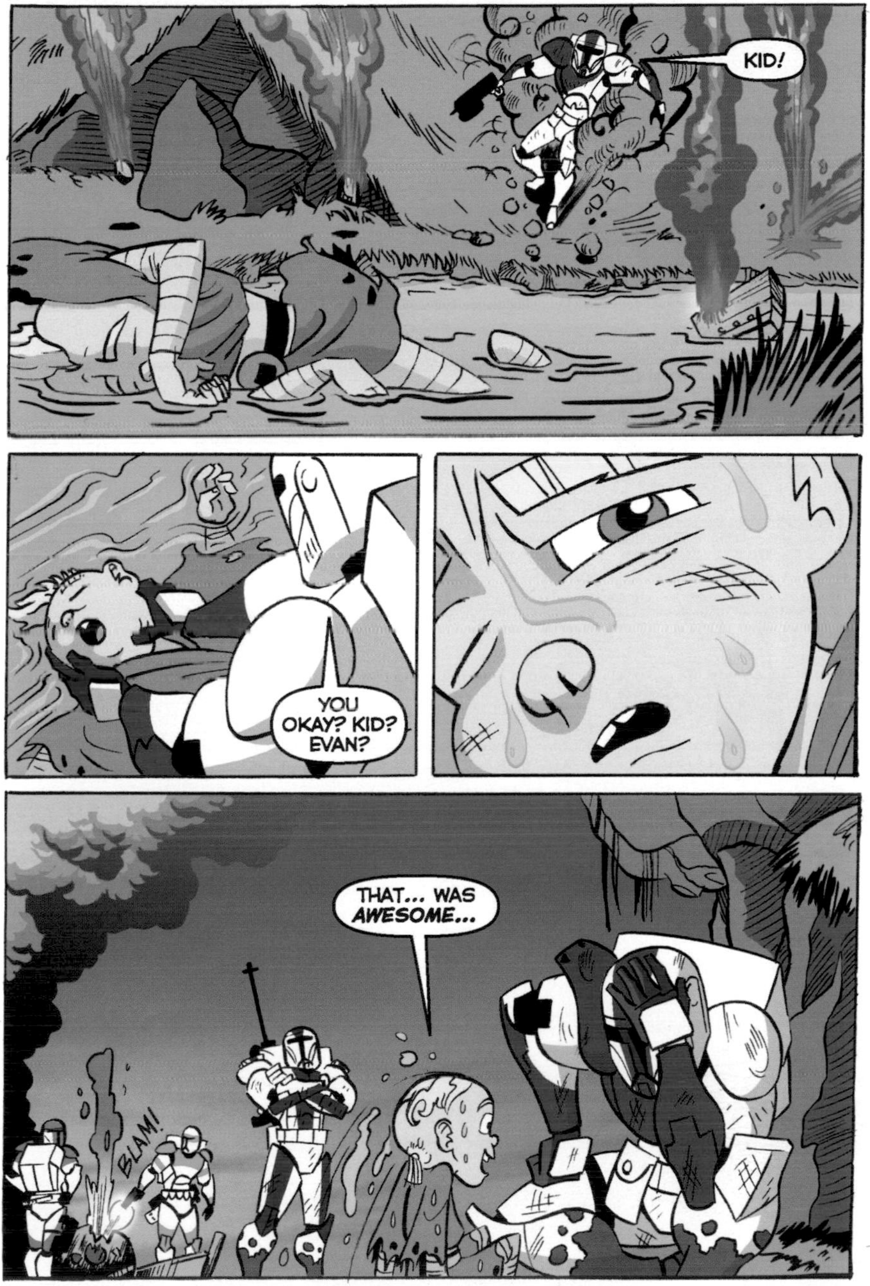
KID!
YOU OKAY? KID? EVAN?
THAT... WAS AWESOME...
BLAM!

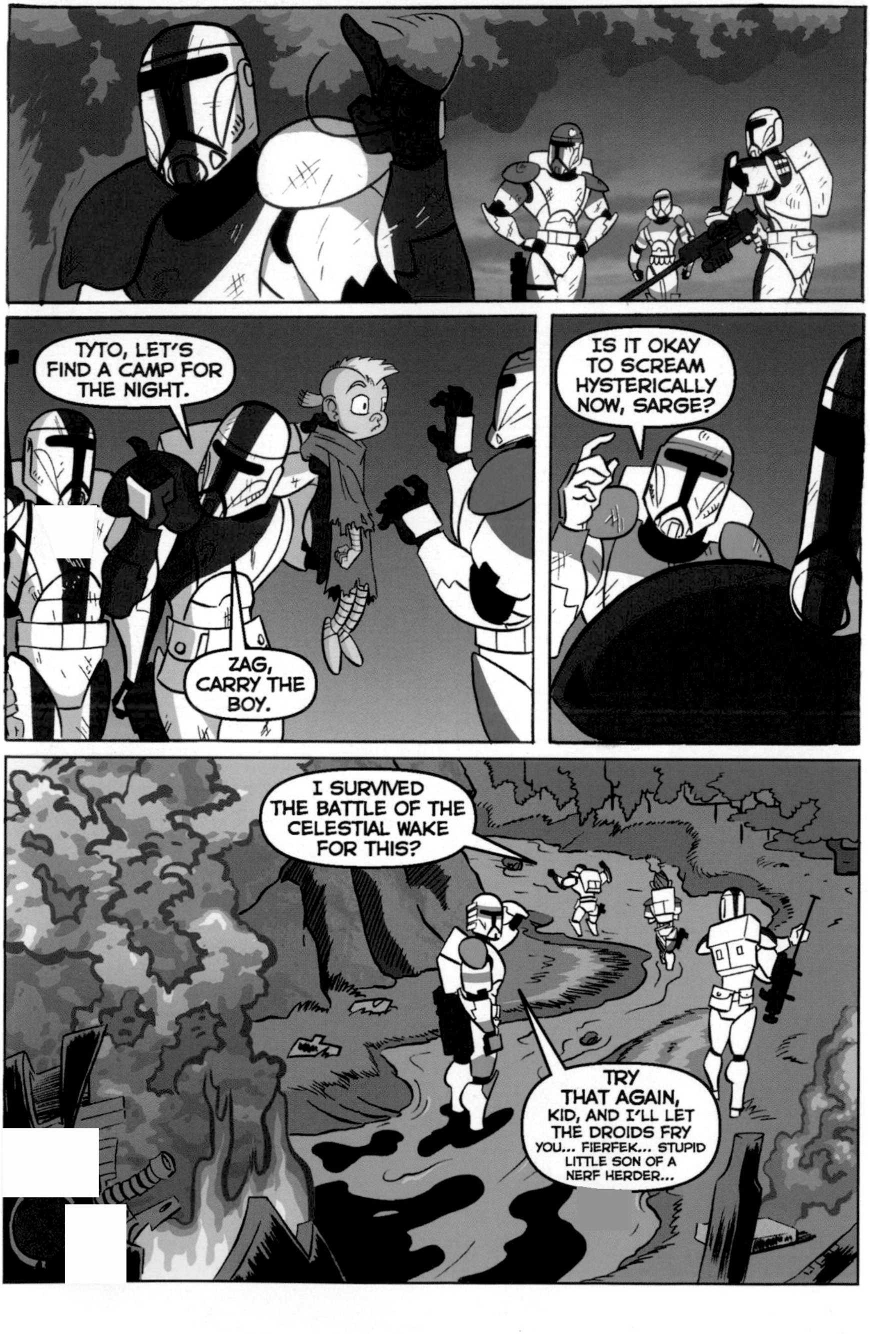
TYTO, LET'S FIND A CAMP FOR THE NIGHT.
ZAG, CARRY THE BOY.
IS IT OKAY TO SCREAM HYSTERICALLY NOW, SARGE?
I SURVIVED THE BATTLE OF THE CELESTIAL WAKE FOR THIS?
TRY THAT AGAIN, KID, AND I'LL LET THE DROIDS FRY YOU... FIERFEK... STUPID LITTLE SON OF A NERF HERDER...

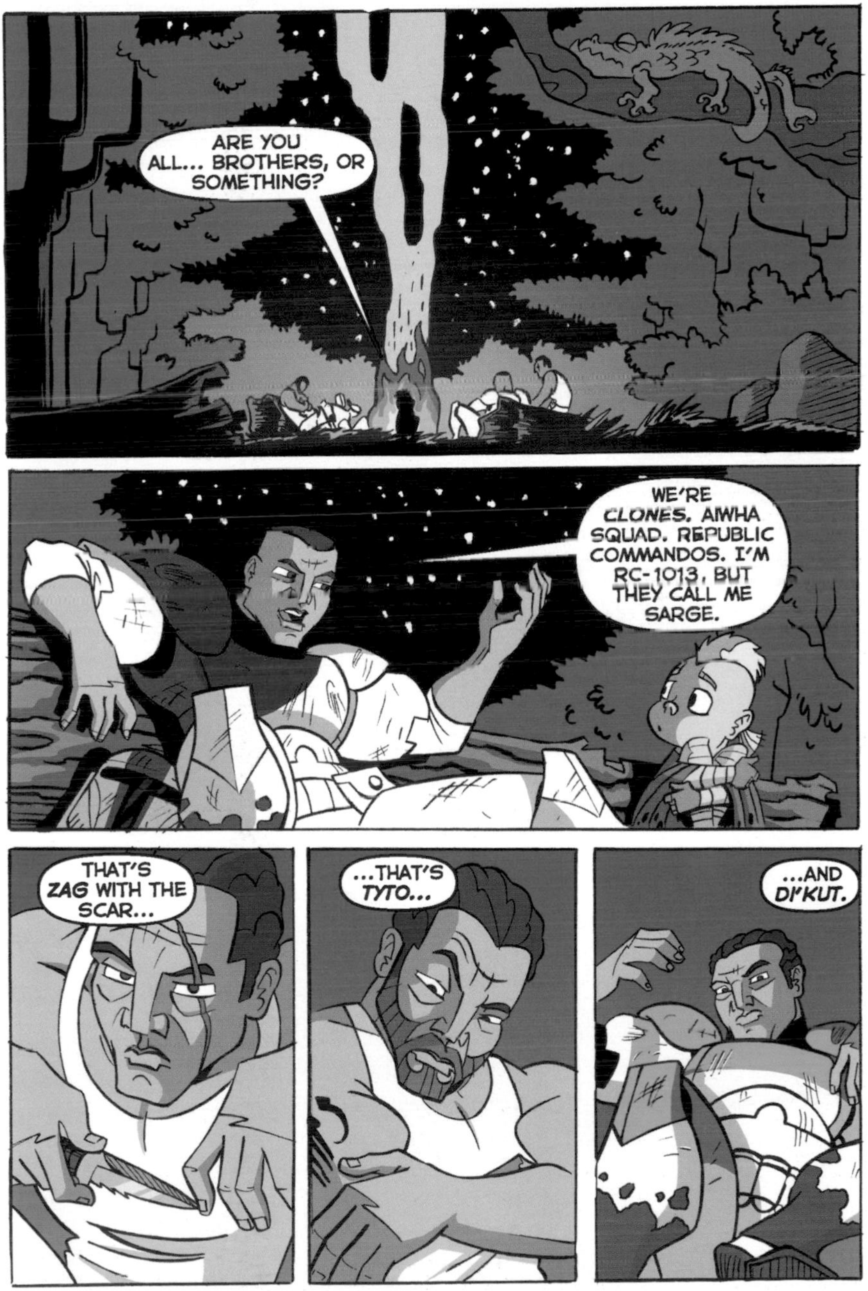
ARE YOU ALL... BROTHERS, OR SOMETHING?
WE'RE *CLONES.* AIWHA SQUAD. REPUBLIC COMMANDOS. I'M RC-1013, BUT THEY CALL ME SARGE.
THAT'S ZAG WITH THE SCAR...
...THAT'S *TYTO*...
...AND *DI'KUT.*

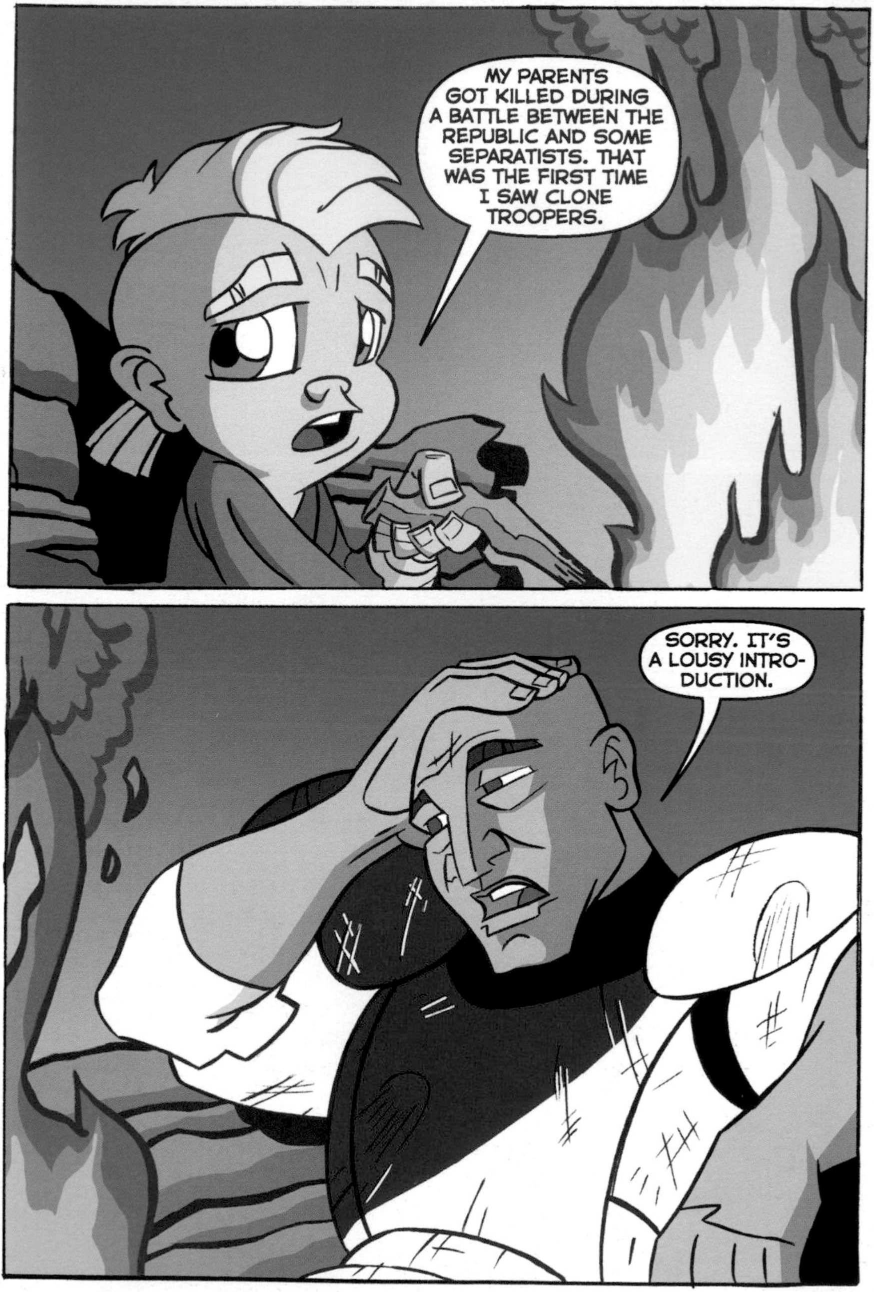
MY PARENTS GOT KILLED DURING A BATTLE BETWEEN THE REPUBLIC AND SOME SEPARATISTS. THAT WAS THE FIRST TIME I SAW CLONE TROOPERS.
SORRY. IT'S A LOUSY INTRO-DUCTION.

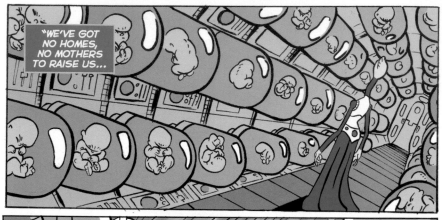

"WE'VE GOT NO HOMES, NO MOTHERS TO RAISE US...

"...NO FATHERS TO GUIDE US...

"...BUT WE WERE THROWN INTO A WAR AND TRAINED TO DIE FOR A REPUBLIC WE'D NEVER EVEN SEEN.

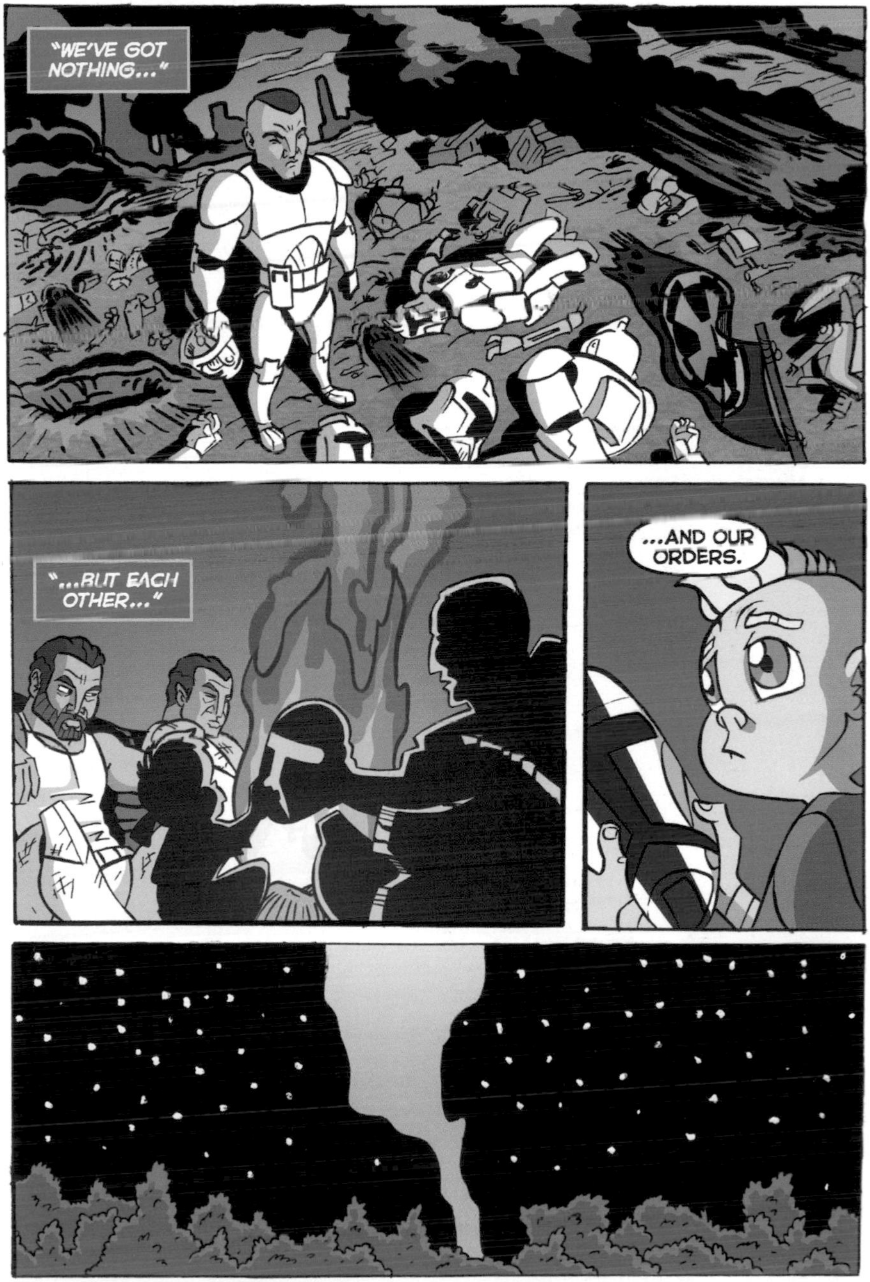
"WE'VE GOT NOTHING..."
"...BUT EACH OTHER..."
...AND OUR ORDERS.

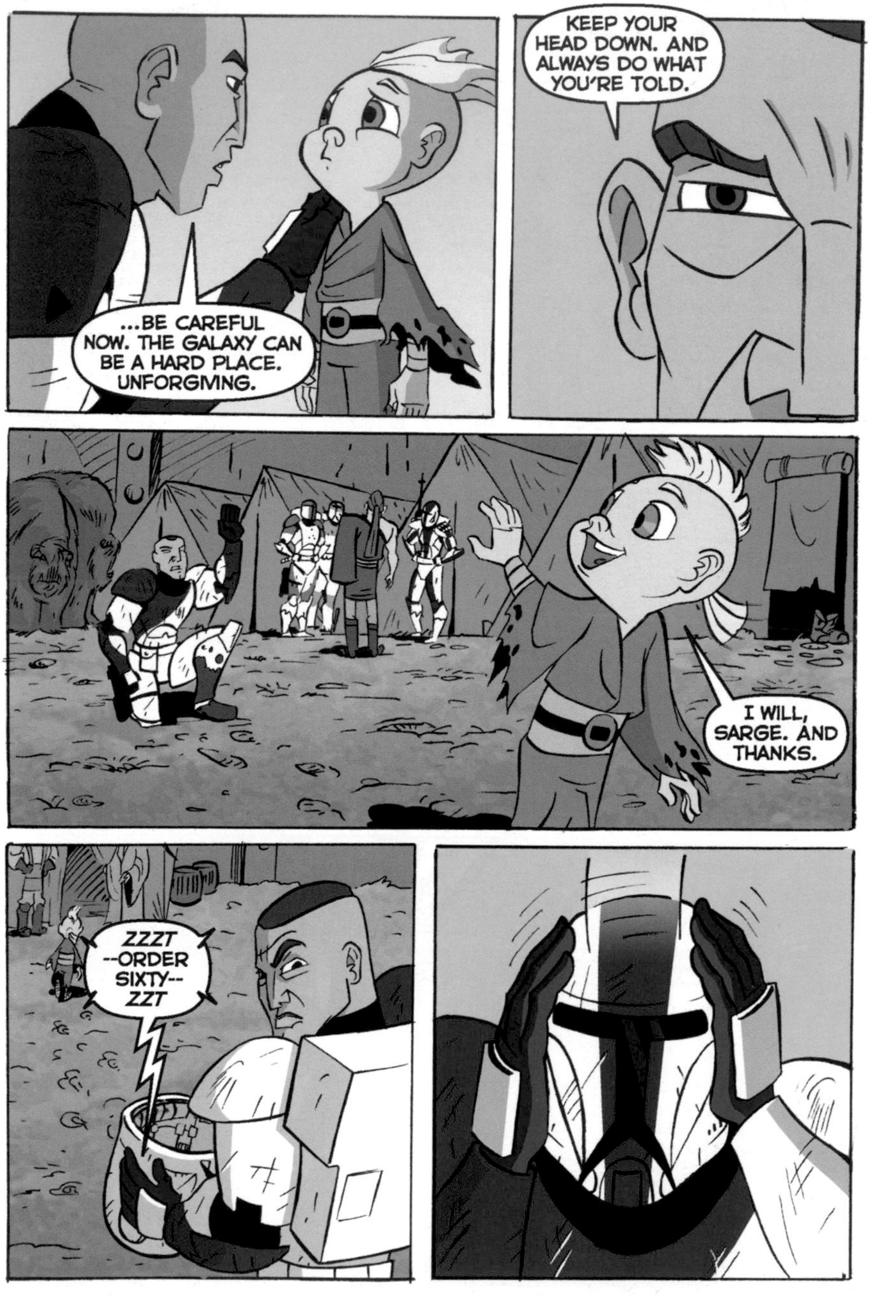
...BE CAREFUL NOW. THE GALAXY CAN BE A HARD PLACE. UNFORGIVING.
KEEP YOUR HEAD DOWN. AND ALWAYS DO WHAT YOU'RE TOLD.
I WILL, SARGE. AND THANKS.
ZZZT --ORDER SIXTY-- ZZT

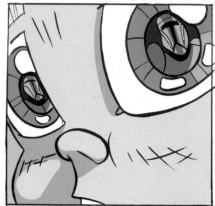

THE JEDI WERE TRAITORS TO THE REPUBLIC. WE FOLLOWED OUR ORDERS.

AND WE DON'T QUESTION ORDERS...

THE END

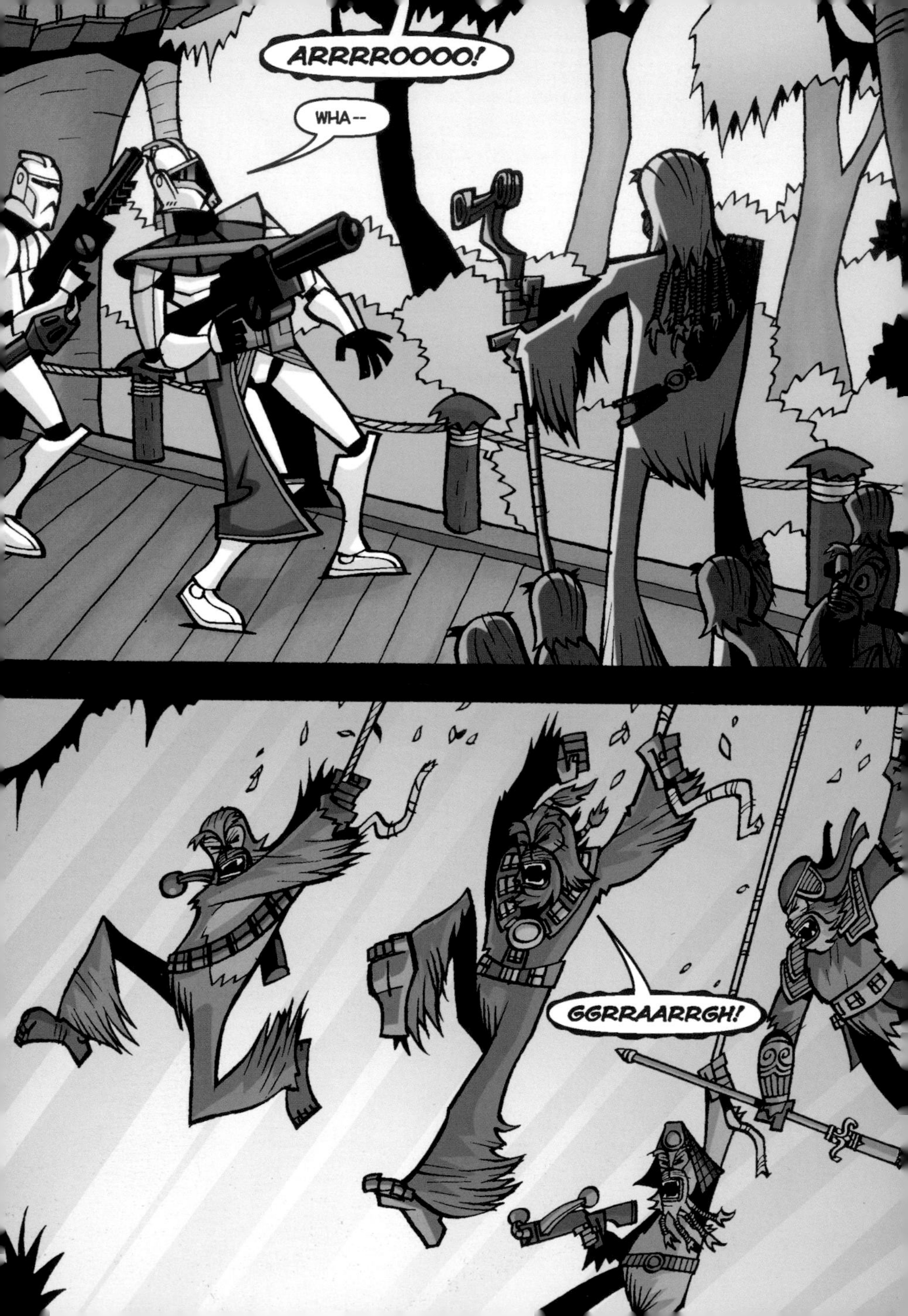
ARRRROOOO!
WHA--
GGRRAARRGH!

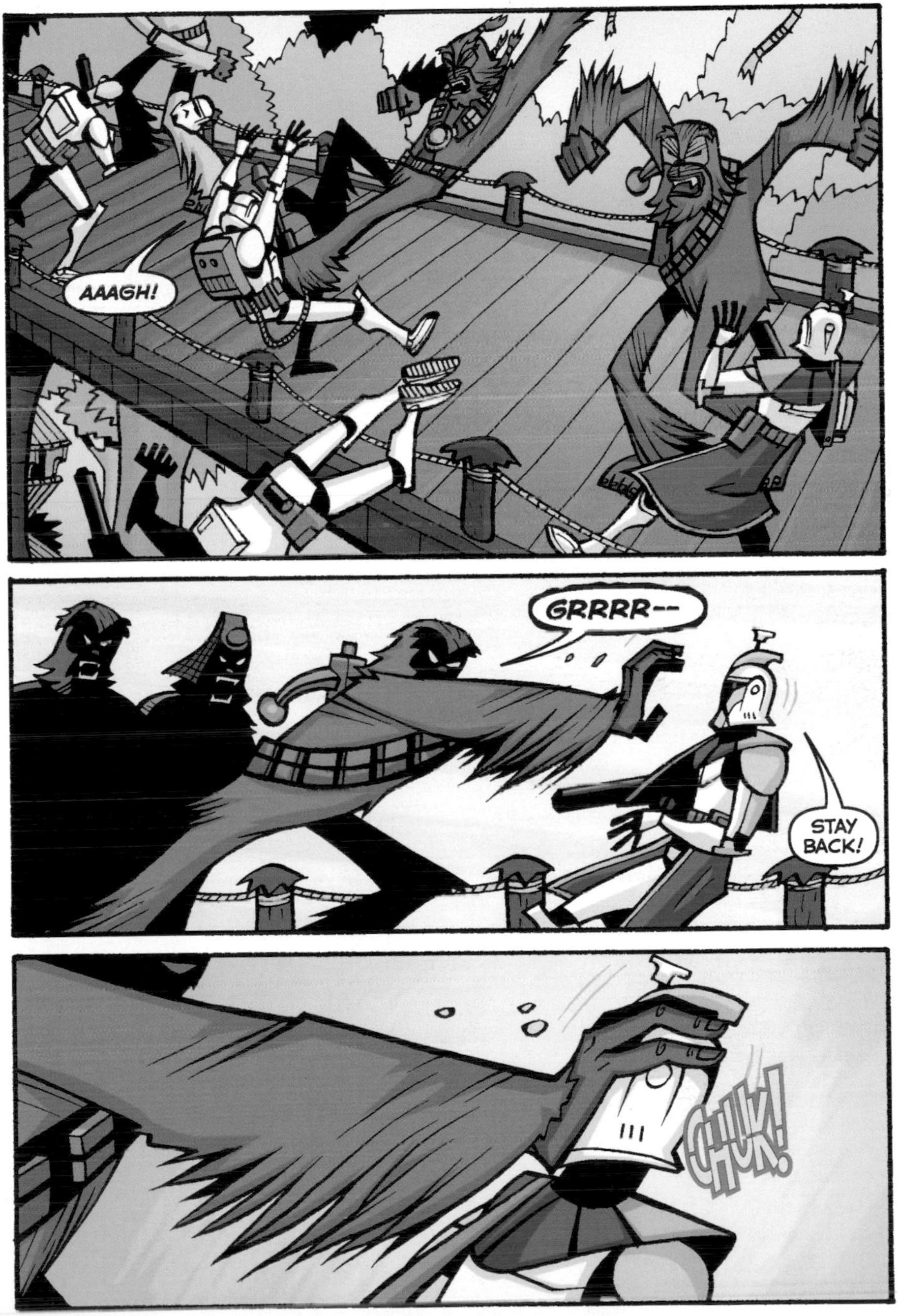
AAAGH!
GRRRR--
STAY BACK!
CHUK!

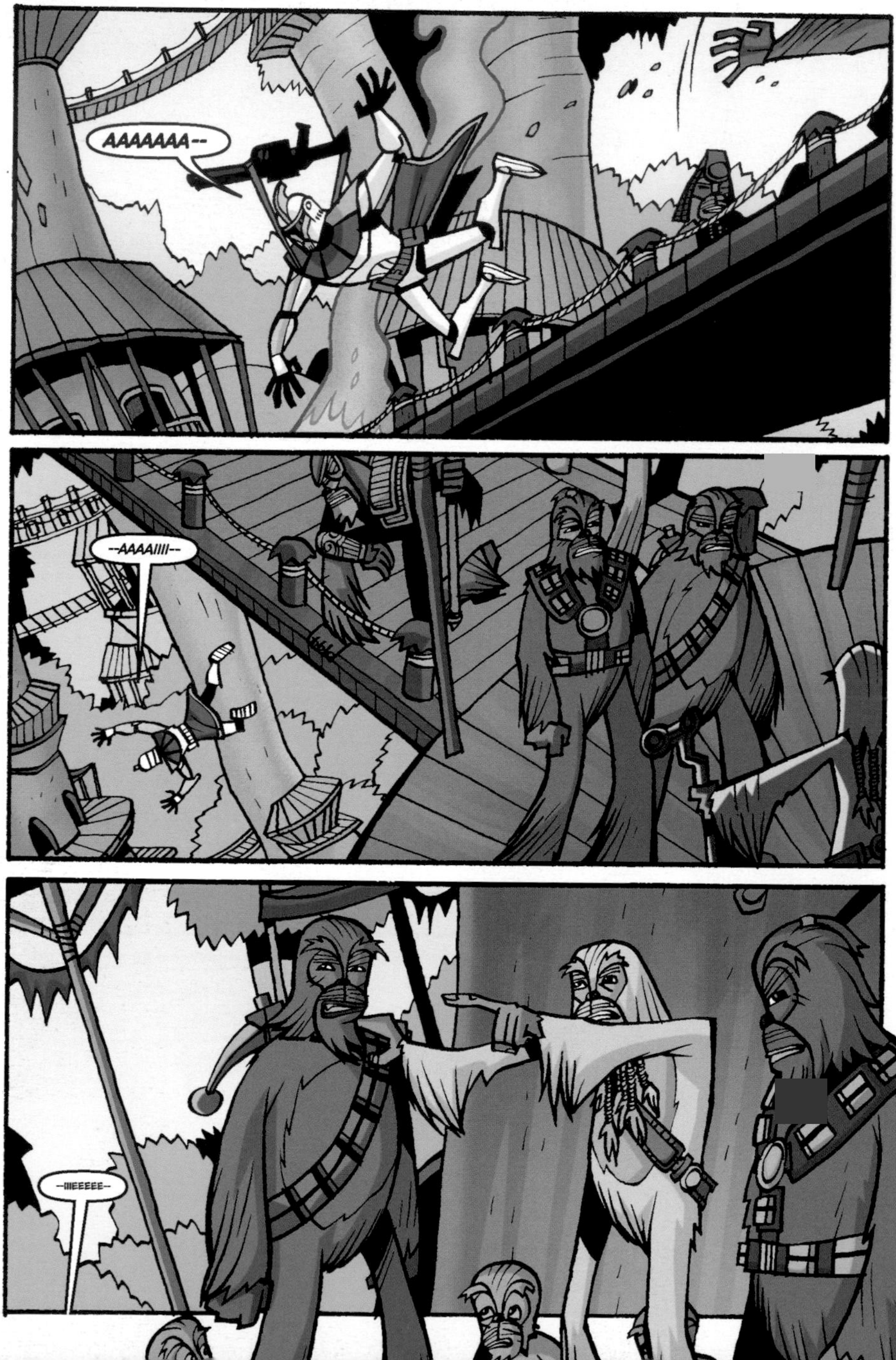
AAAAAAA--
--AAAAIIII--
--IIIEEEEEE--

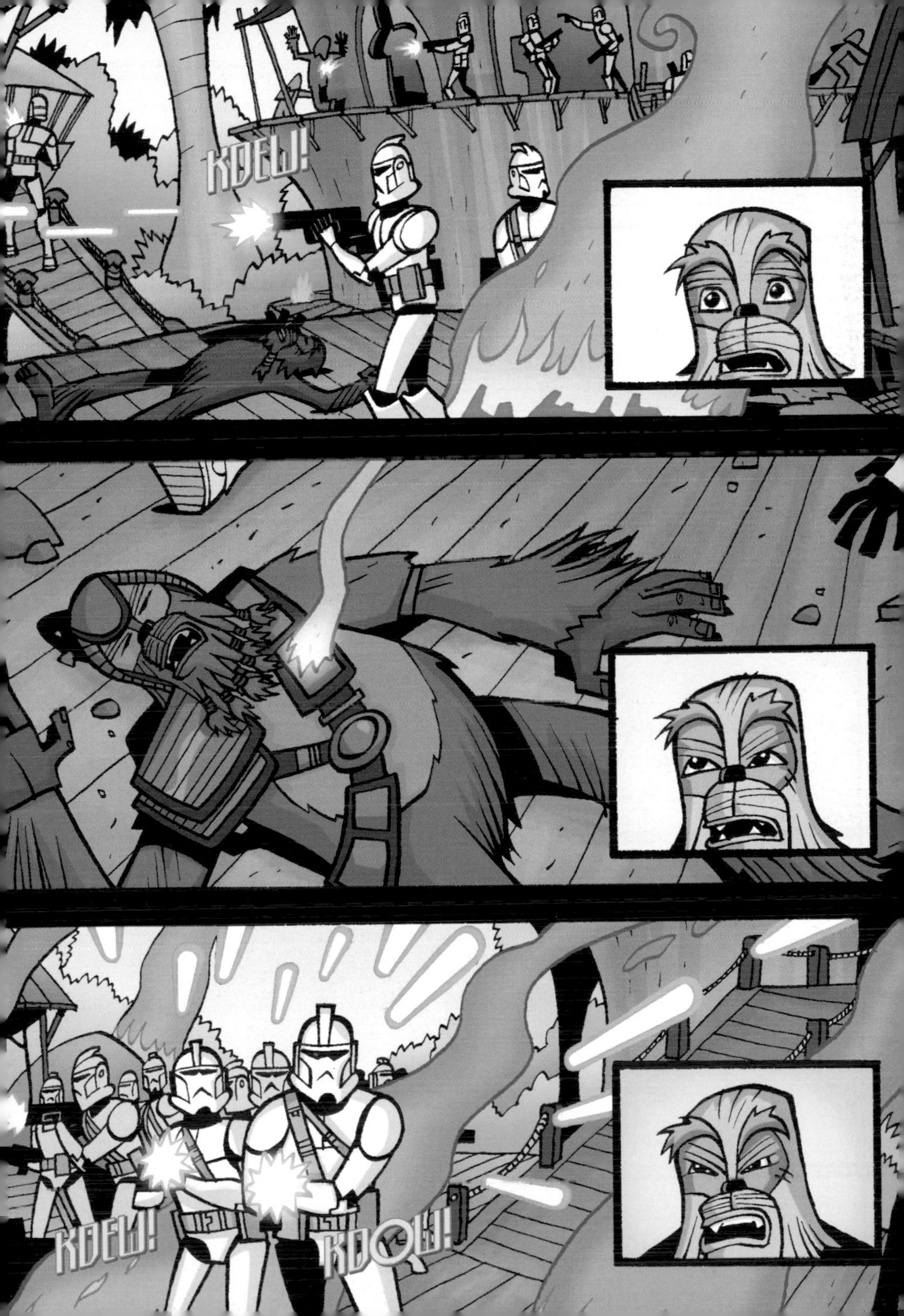
KDEW!
KDEW!
KDOW!

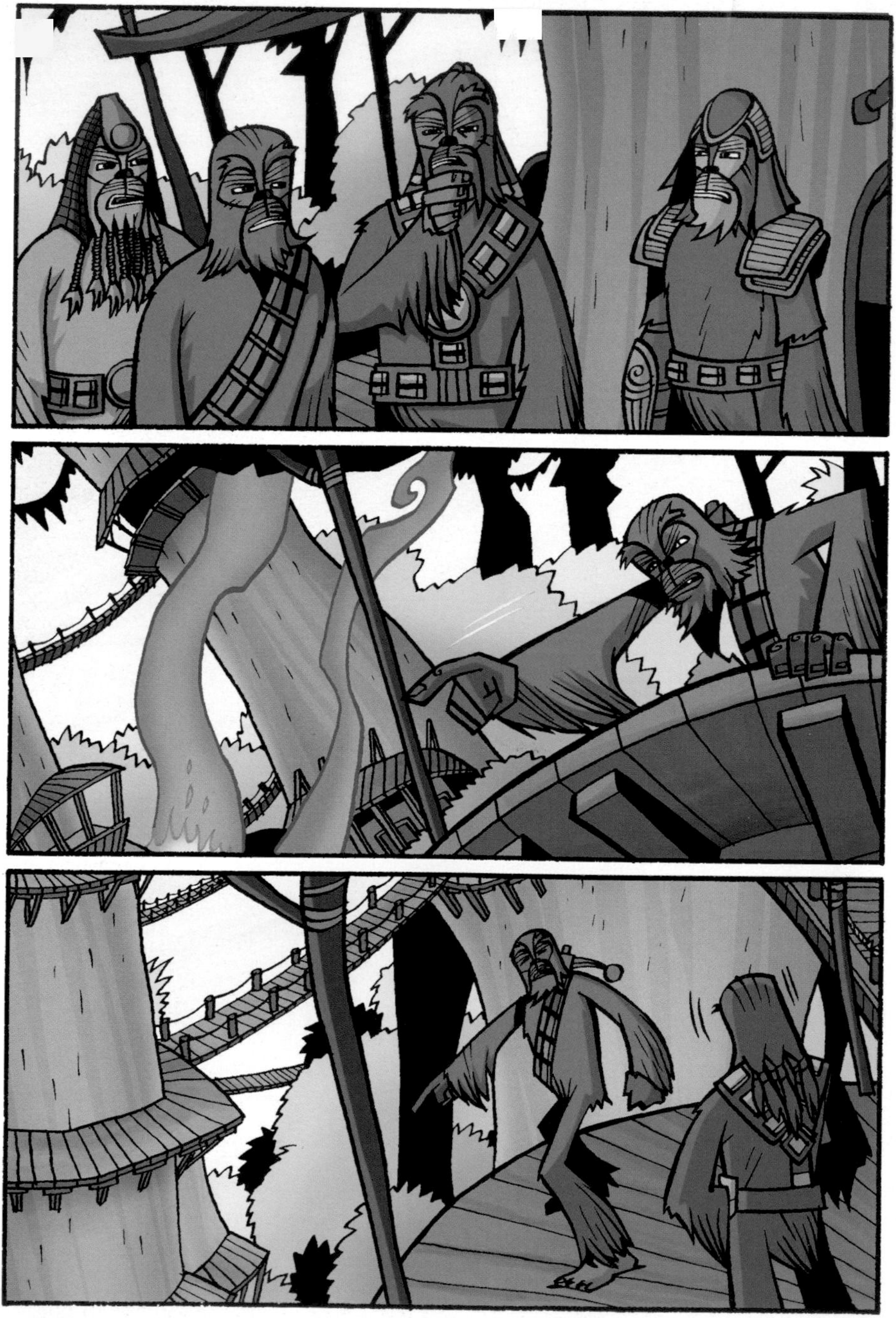

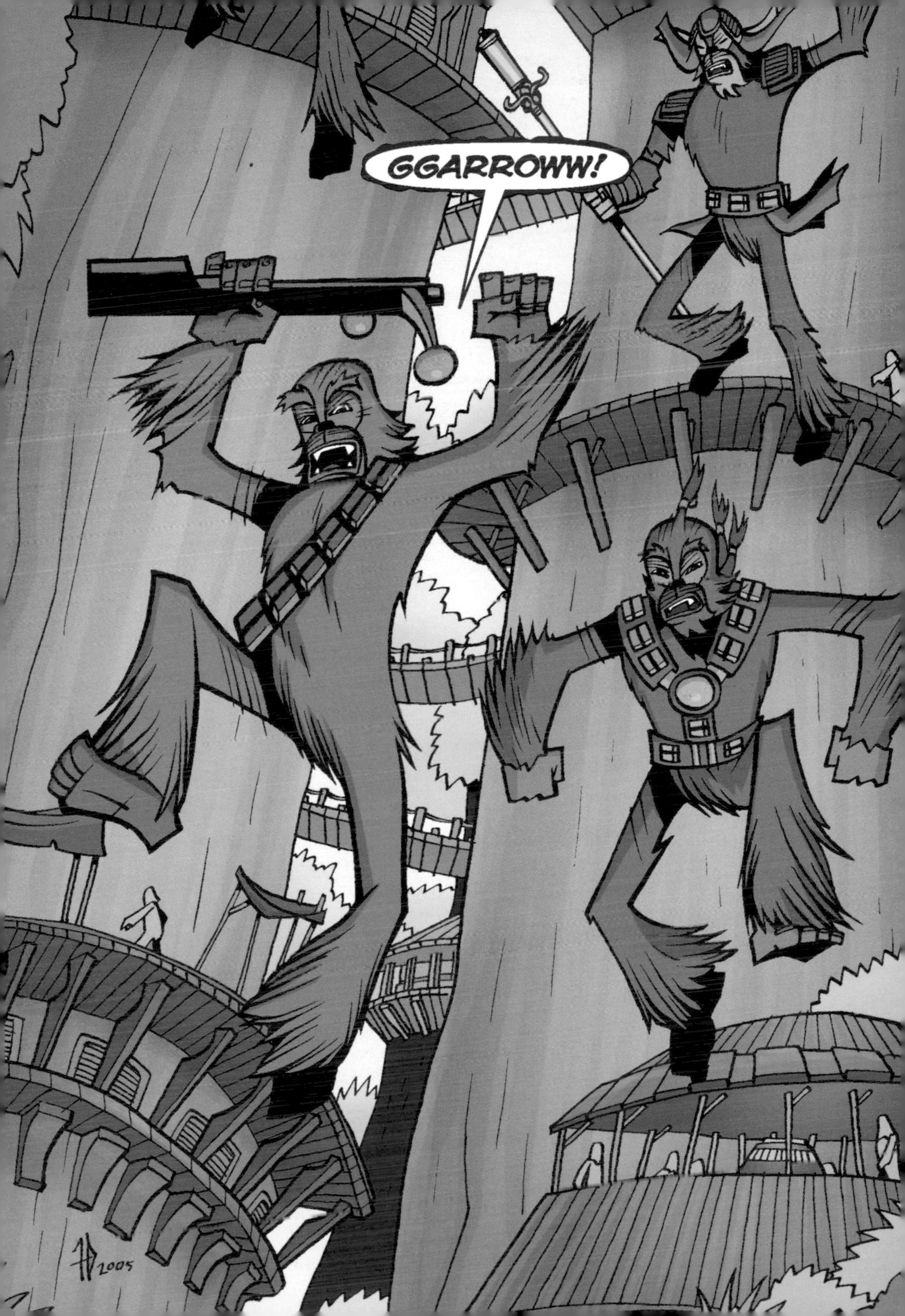
GGARROWW!
2005

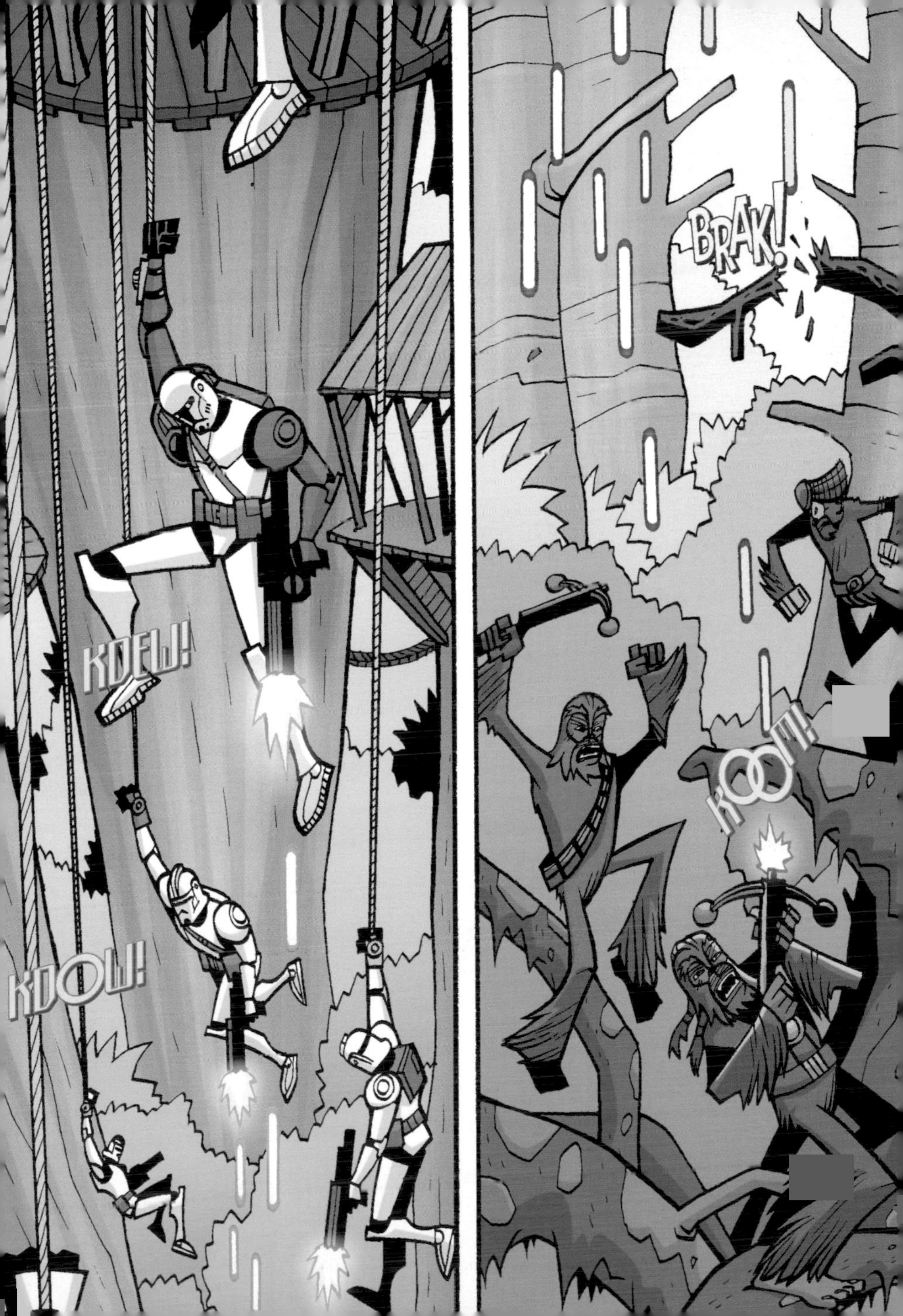
KDEW!
KDOW!
BRAK!
KOOM!

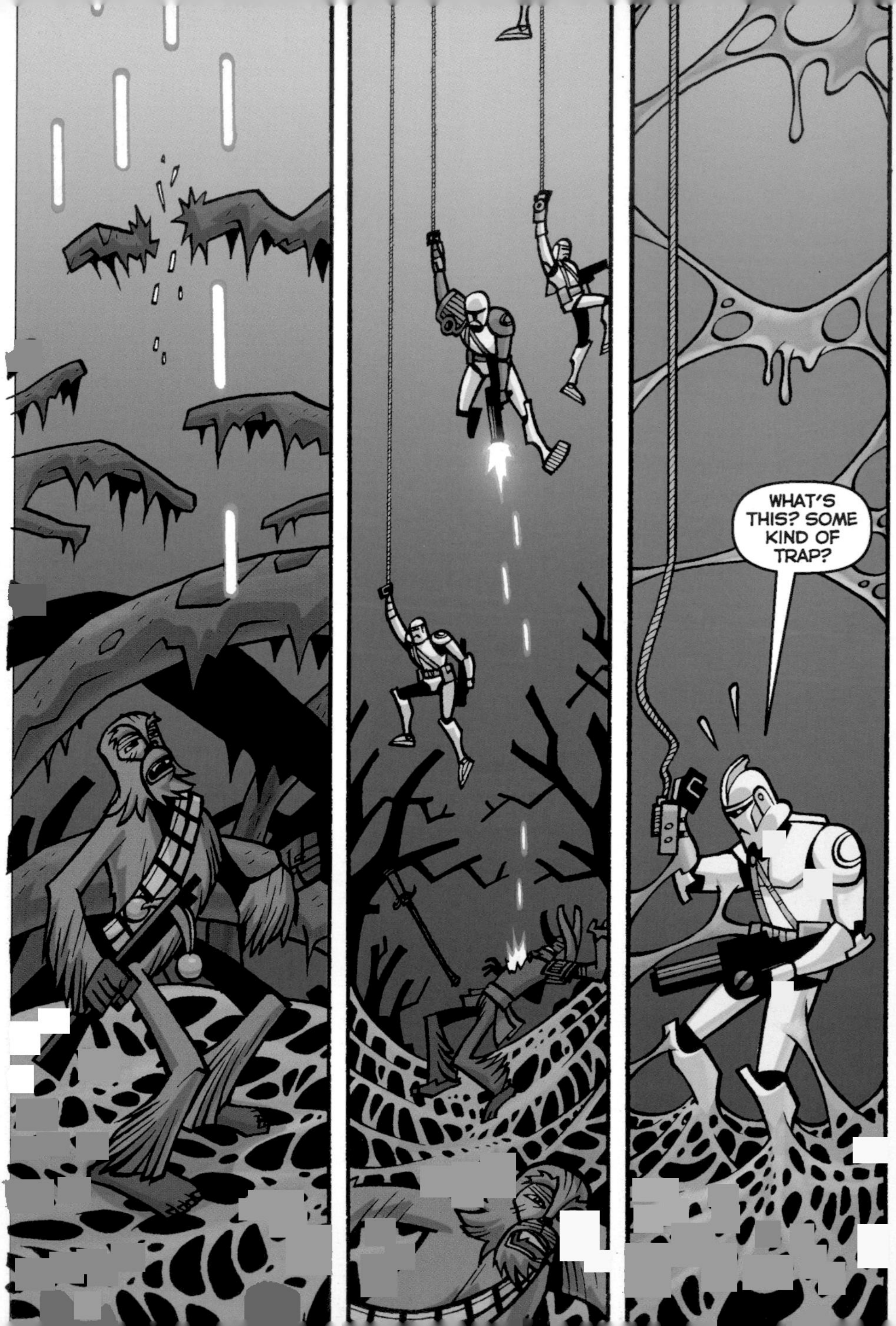
WHAT'S THIS? SOME KIND OF TRAP?

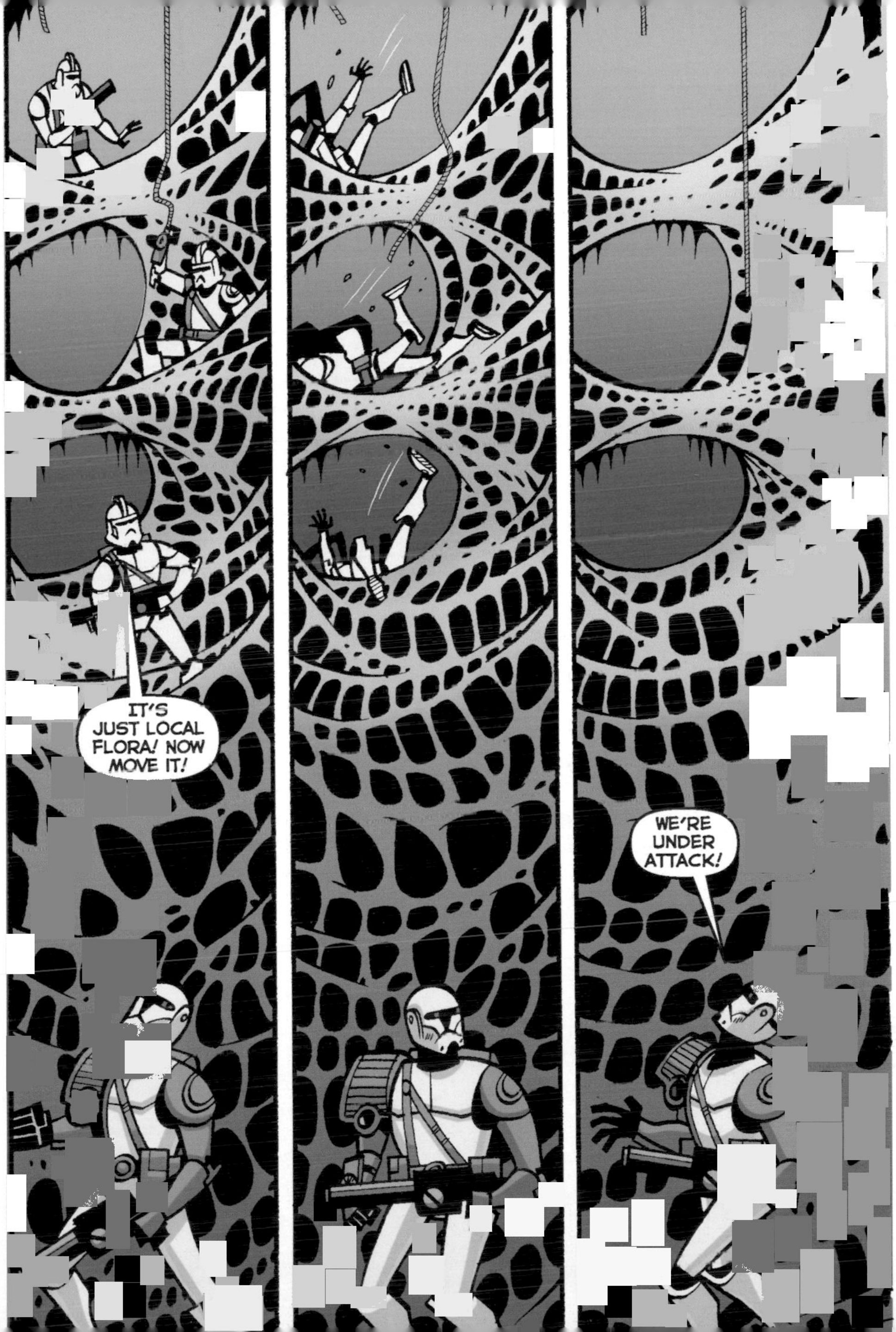
IT'S JUST LOCAL FLORA! NOW MOVE IT!
WE'RE UNDER ATTACK!

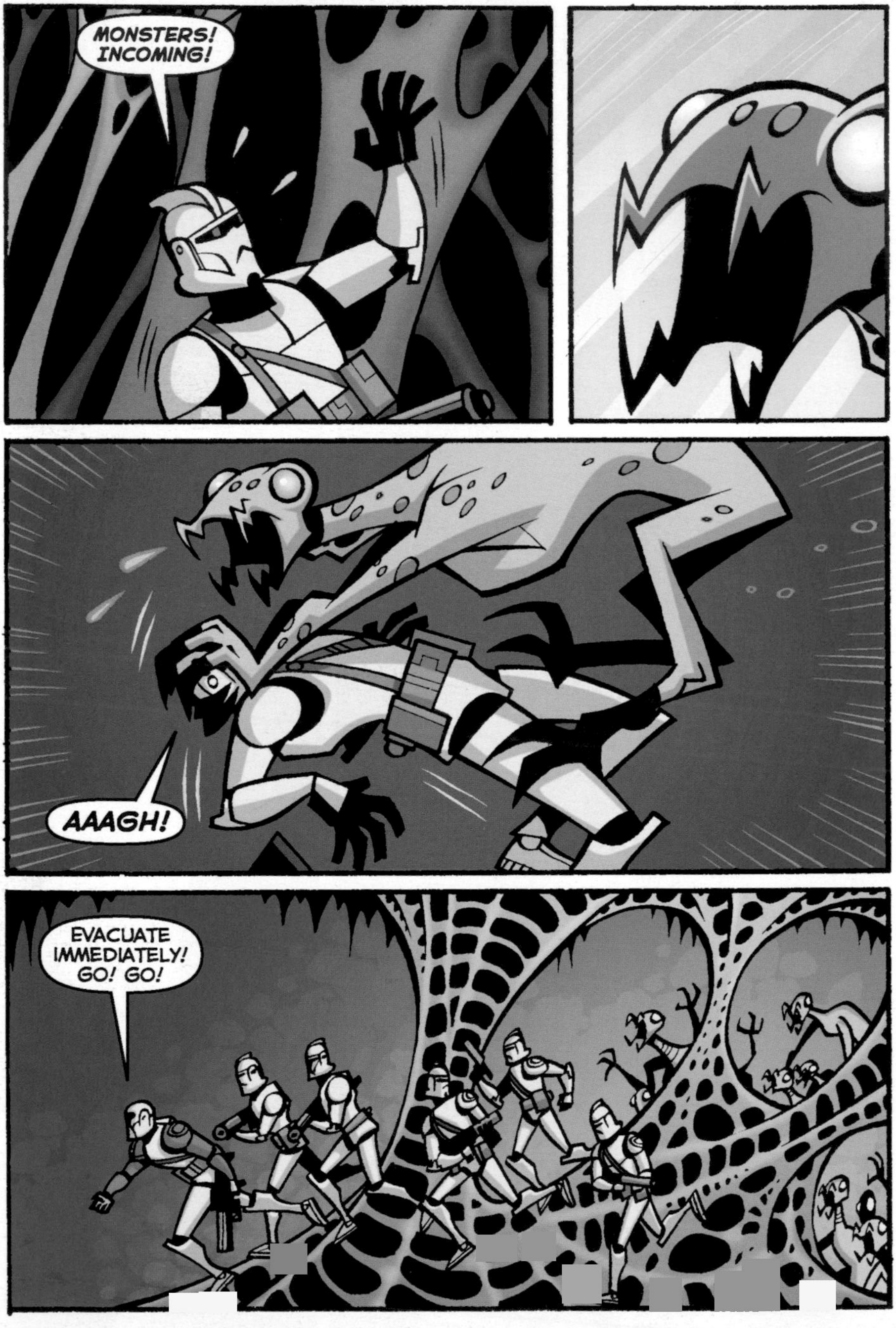
MONSTERS! INCOMING!
AAAGH!
EVACUATE IMMEDIATELY! GO! GO!

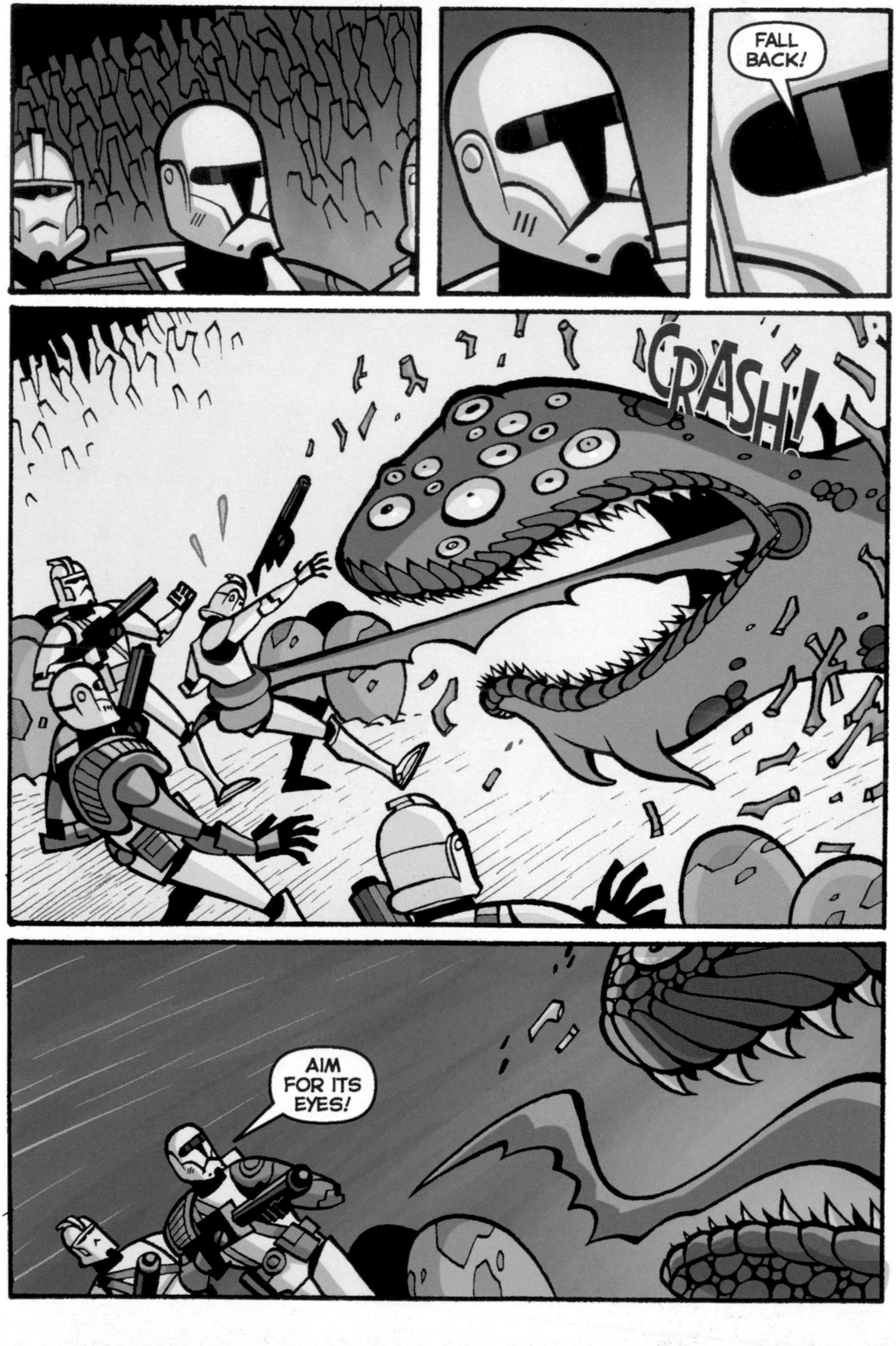
FALL BACK!
CRASH!
AIM FOR ITS EYES!

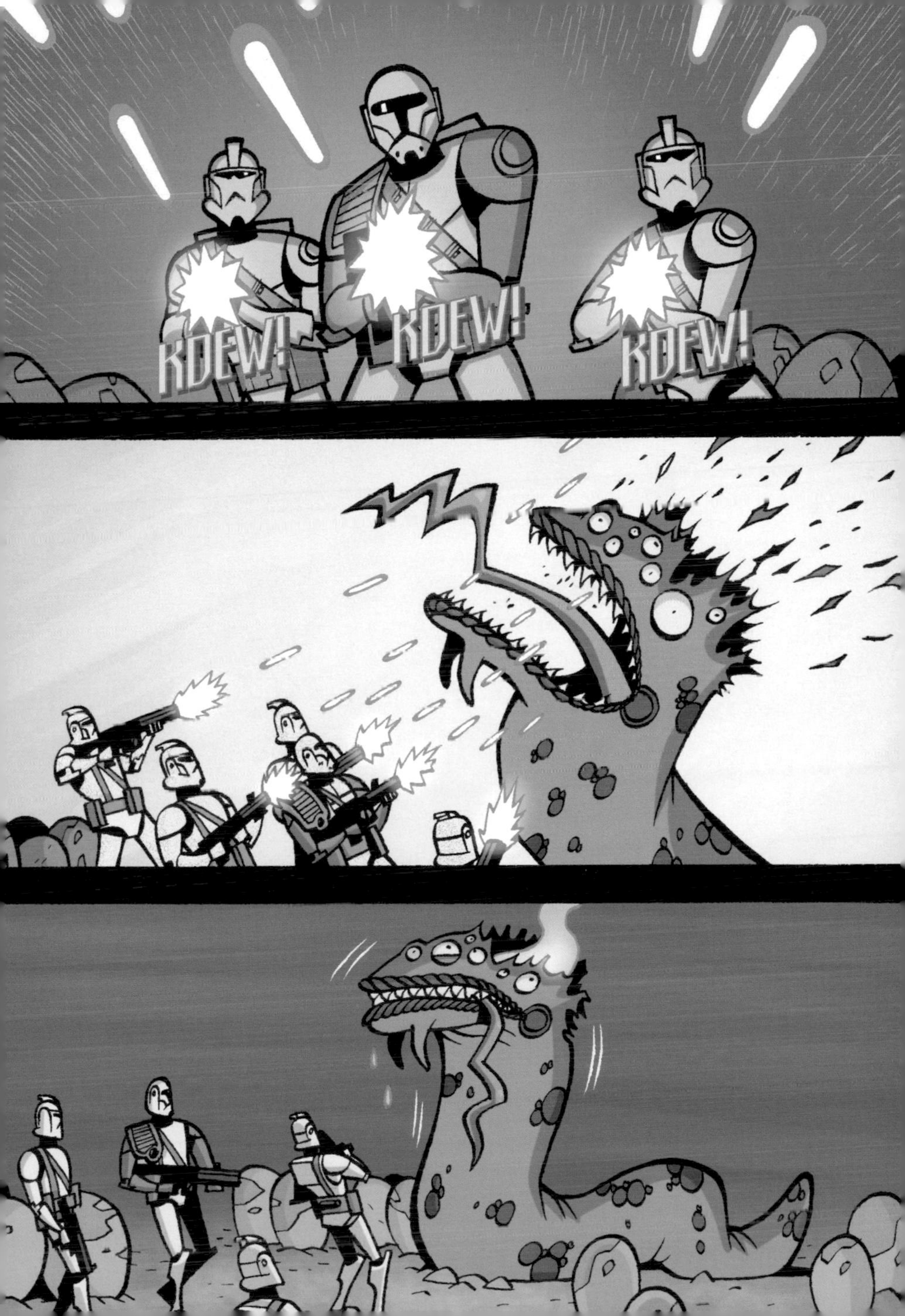
KDEW!
KDEW!
KDEW!

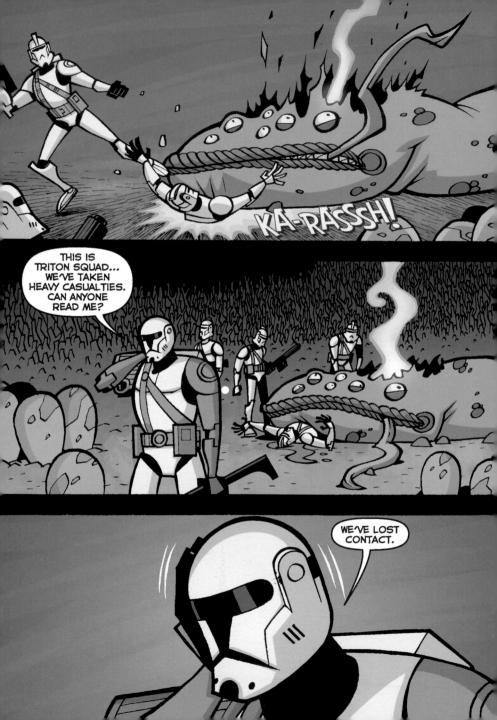

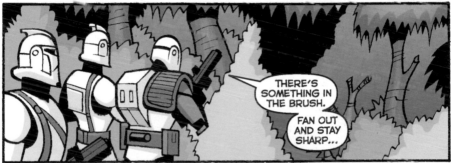

THERE'S SOMETHING IN THE BRUSH.

FAN OUT AND STAY SHARP...

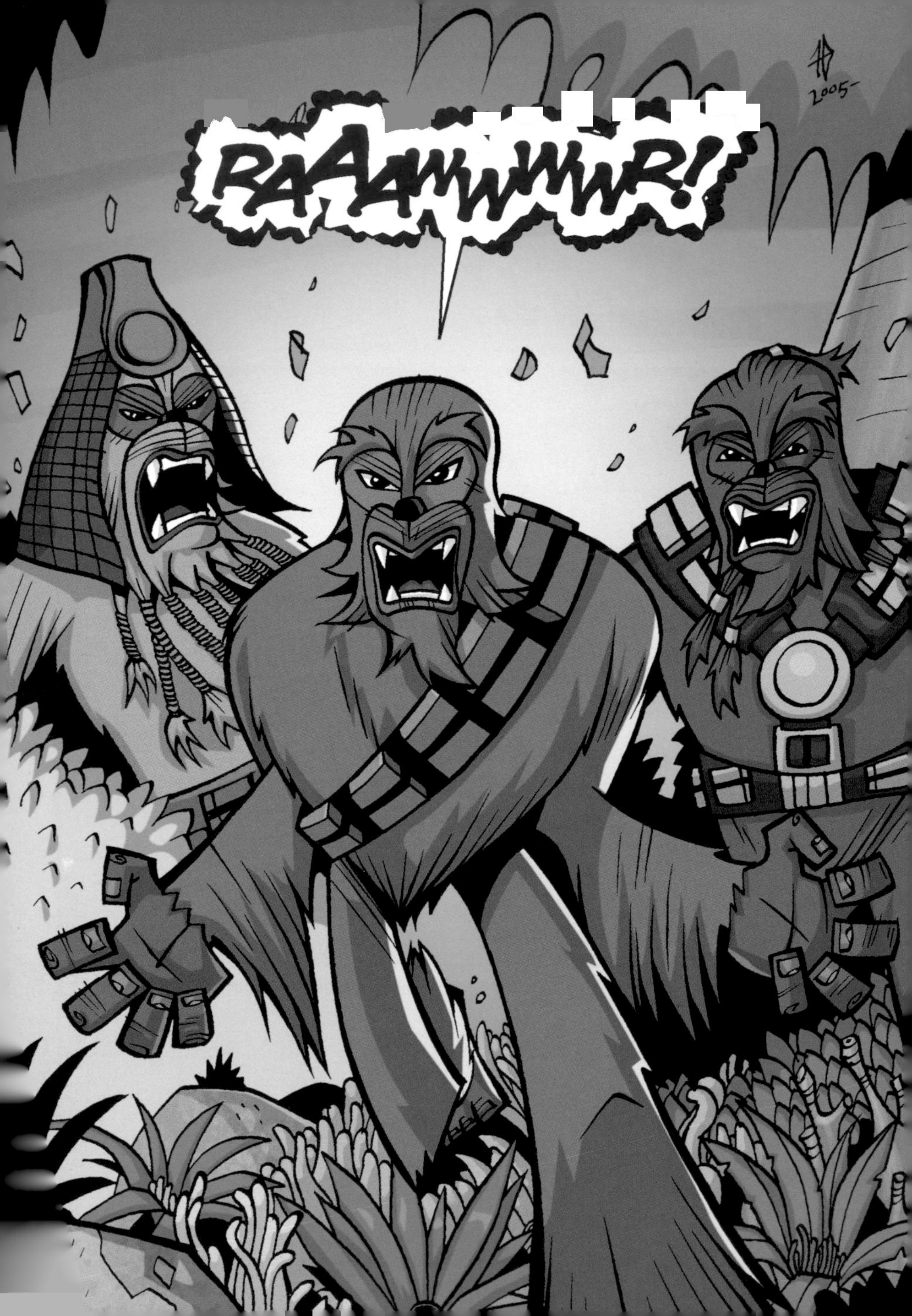
RAAAWWWR!

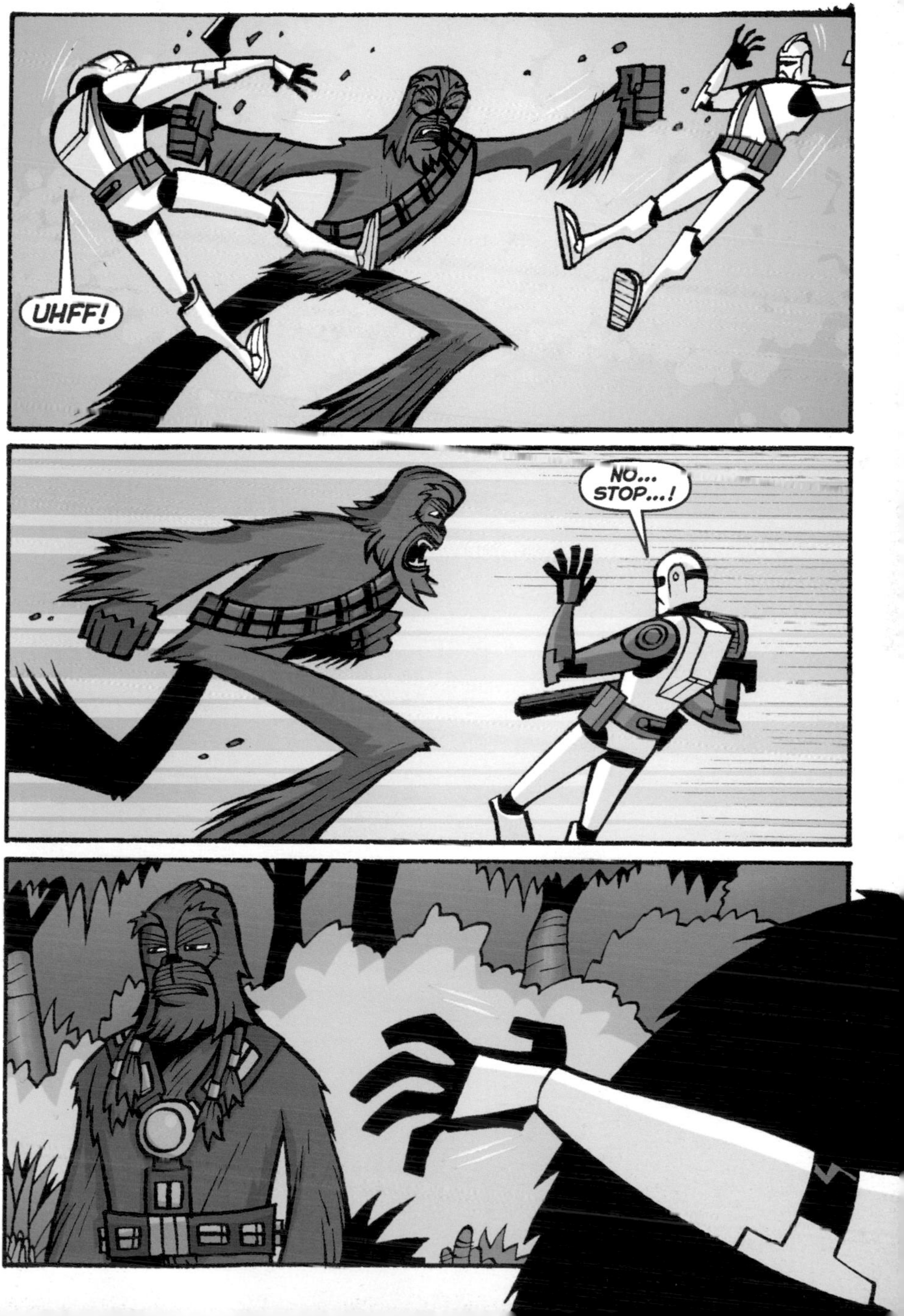
UHFF!
NO... STOP...!

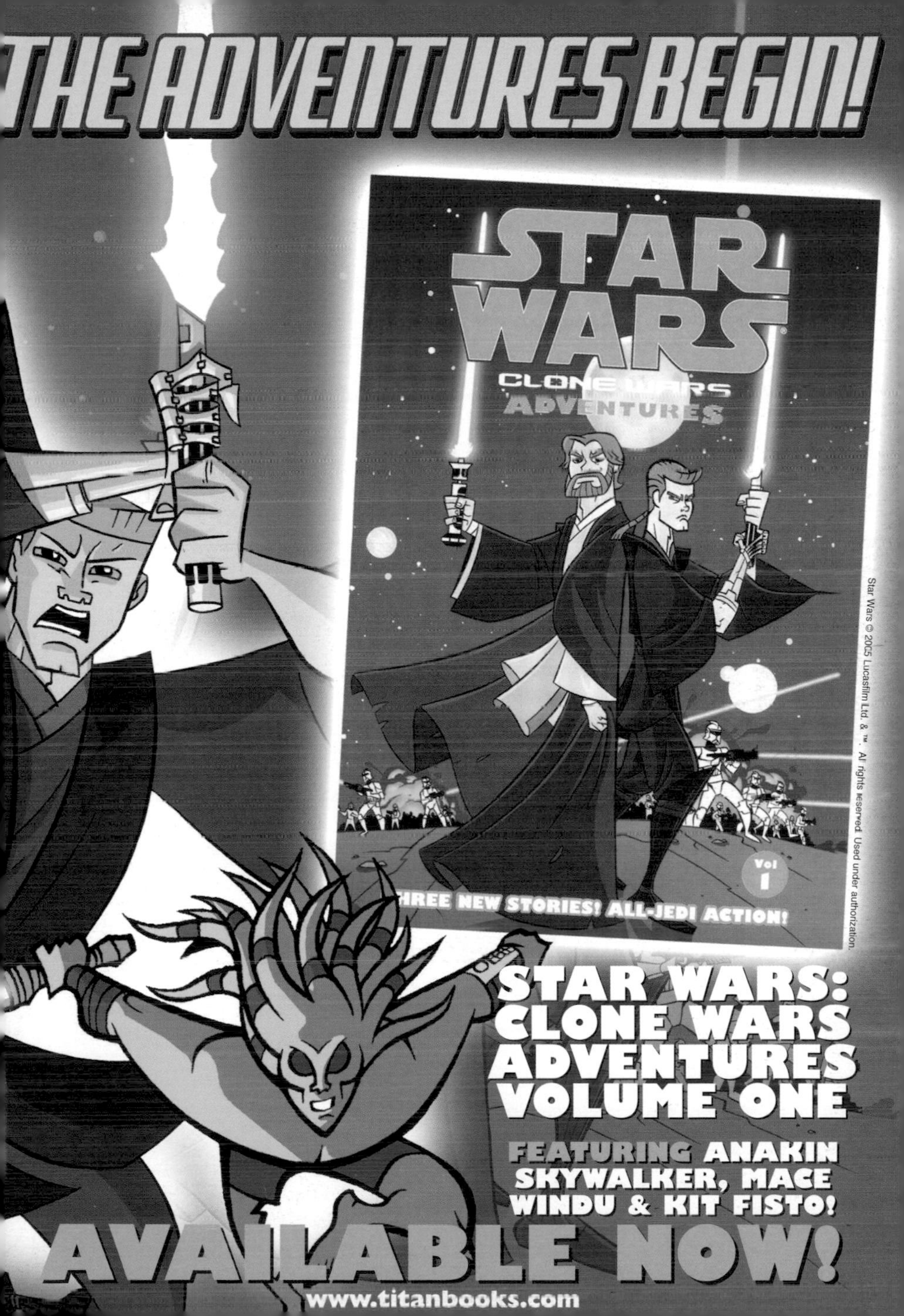
THE ADVENTURES BEGIN!
STAR WARS
CLONE WARS
ADVENTURES
Vol 1
THREE NEW STORIES! ALL-JEDI ACTION!
Star Wars © 2005 Lucasfilm Ltd. & ™. All rights reserved. Used under authorization.
STAR WARS: CLONE WARS ADVENTURES VOLUME ONE
FEATURING ANAKIN SKYWALKER, MACE WINDU & KIT FISTO!
AVAILABLE NOW!
www.titanbooks.com

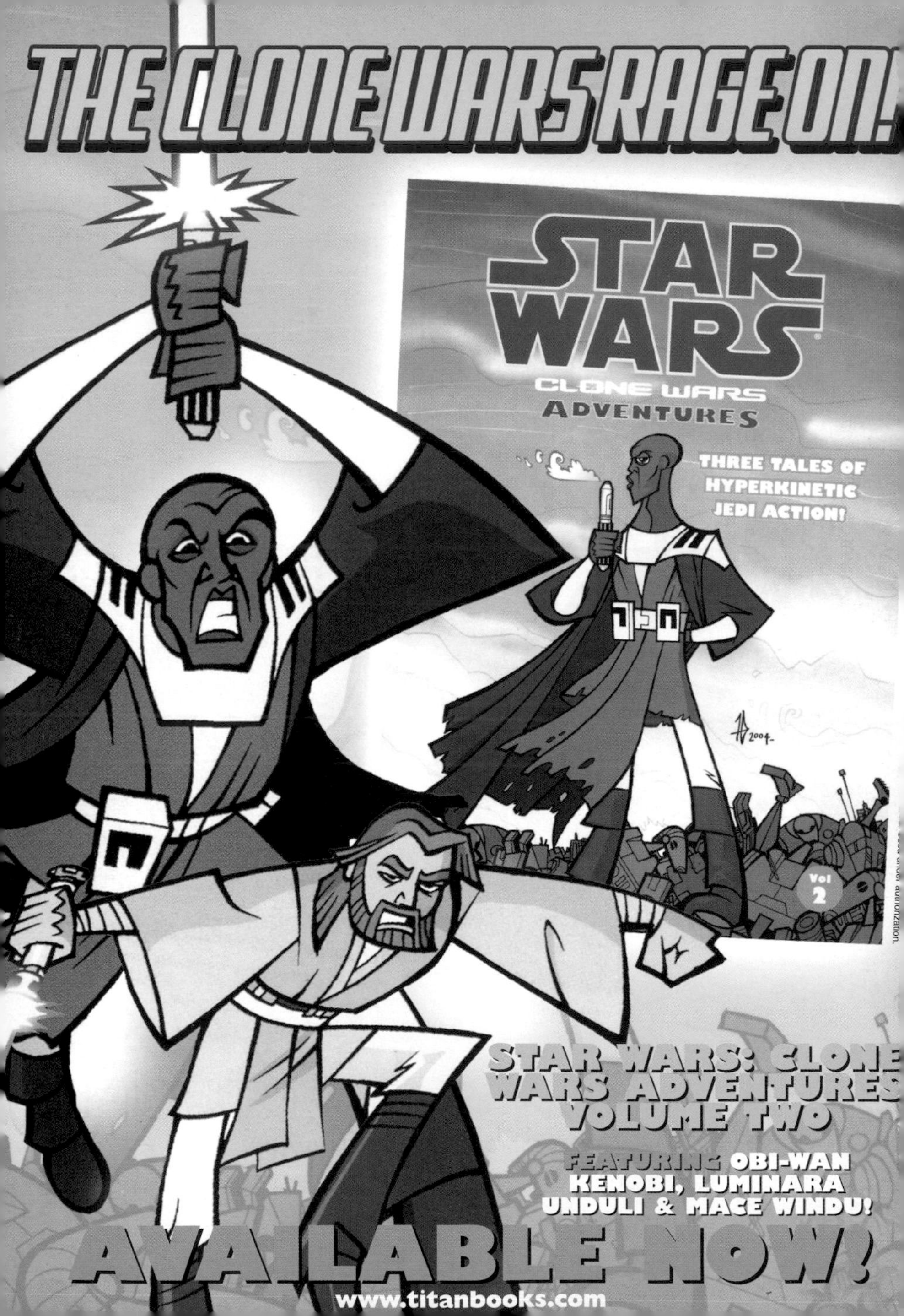
THE CLONE WARS RAGE ON!
STAR WARS
CLONE WARS
ADVENTURES
THREE TALES OF HYPERKINETIC JEDI ACTION!
Vol 2
STAR WARS: CLONE WARS ADVENTURES VOLUME TWO
FEATURING OBI-WAN KENOBI, LUMINARA UNDULI & MACE WINDU!
AVAILABLE NOW!
www.titanbooks.com